How to Become a Barrister

Mark Andrews

ISBN: 978-1-910662-33-5

First published 2016

Contents

'THE BARRISTER' 1

AREAS OF WORK 19

IS THE JOB RIGHT FOR ME? 27

A BARRISTER'S PERSPECTIVE 37

ENTRY REQUIREMENTS 53

REGULATION AND CONTINUED PROFESSIONAL DEVELOPMENT 71

BAR COURSE APTITUDE TEST (BCAT) 77

IMPROVING YOUR CHANCES 115

CREATING YOUR CV 123

THE APPLICATION FORM 137

THE INTERVIEW 161

GLOSSARY AND KEY TERMS 185

INTRODUCTION

Welcome, to the ultimate guide to becoming a barrister. This guide has been written with the sole intention to help, advise and prepare people who are thinking about a career as a barrister.

This demanding and complex profession is proven to be a highly sought after career, of which only the best of the best will succeed. Packed full of useful information and top tips, this guide focuses on the role of a barrister, the areas of work in the legal industry, the educational qualifications required, career opportunities available, and how to achieve and maintain a successful career as a UK barrister.

Becoming a barrister requires high levels of professionalism, skill and commitment. Not everyone will be suited to the role of a barrister, and it takes a unique individual to maintain a strong, successful, legal career. Do you have what it takes to maintain such a career? Well, if you think the answer is yes, this book will act as your go-to guide and help you on your journey to becoming a UK barrister.

This guide will deliver invaluable information that will allow you to take your first steps in a long, stressful and competitive journey. If you want to become a barrister, then you will need to understand the expectations and demanding nature of the profession. You need to be aware that this profession should not be entered into light-heartedly. The selection process requires extreme levels of hard work, motivation and passion, and thus it is important to ask yourself 'whether this chosen career is right for you'. I was fortunate enough to spend over a decade working with barristers. I watched and observed their encapsulating performances in court; whether it was a high profile murder trial or a human rights case, I was continuously impressed with the ability to argue and articulate delicate, and often complex, points of law in front of a judge and jury. Their performances would keep everyone in the court room enthralled and hanging on their every word. The fact is, barristers are an integral part of the legal profession, and without whom the legal industry would not be the same. This is one of many reasons that I was interested in writing this career guide – I wanted to ensure that the next generation of 'would-be barristers' would never be put off by the hurdles in the way to qualifying and practising in court as a barrister.

In this book you will learn all of the important aspects of the role of a barrister, and how to achieve a successful, legal career. This unique guide has been carefully broken up into specific chapters, in order for you to make the most out of your learning and preparation.

This guide will:

- Help you decide whether this job is right for you, and also, whether you are right for the job;
- Allow you to understand the important stages of the selection process and what is expected;
- Give you a step-by-step guide through the application process and everything you need to know in terms of education, skills,

qualifications and experience;

- Give you an insight into what the Chambers are looking for in terms of potential barristers and future prospects;
- Assist you through the interview stage of your pupillage, and show sample questions that you are likely to encounter;
- Provide tips and advice throughout, in order to help you on your pursuit to becoming a barrister.

This guide primarily focuses on providing vital information so that you can make informed decisions regarding the choices available.

Taking the first steps into your future as a barrister starts right here. Take your time, read through the guide, and consider whether or not a career as a barrister is right for you.

Remember, work hard, believe in yourself, and success will come your way!

CHAPTER 1

'THE BARRISTER'

The legal profession is made up of many different types of people. From judges to magistrates, solicitors to barristers; they all serve within the legal sector, and they all practice the law in different ways.

Now, it may sound silly and I do not want to insult your intelligence, but before we move on to the more *'juicy'* aspects of the job role, it is important that you know what we actually mean by the term 'barrister'. How does this differ from other legal professions such as magistrates and solicitors? How do you know whether to become a barrister or enter the legal industry through another profession? All these questions are perfectly normal, and it may take you a while to get your head around what career you actually want.

Within this chapter, I am going to discuss the role of a barrister, in order to answer some of those initial questions you might have. I would advise that you take some notes throughout this section, and think about whether you see yourself in this type of role. As we work through this chapter, ask yourself the following questions:

- What do you want to achieve in your career?
- What kind of lawyer do you want to be?
- Why do you want to join the legal industry?
- Where do your strengths lie?
- What are your weaknesses?
- Have you considered other legal careers such as a solicitor?
- What makes the role of a barrister stand out?
- Do you have what it takes to achieve this dream?

WHAT IS A BARRISTER?

A barrister is an individual who works in the legal profession and is usually involved in advocacy and litigation in court. In the UK, barristers are different to solicitors in that they have less initial contact with their clients. Barristers are admitted to the Bar of England and Wales and can work in this jurisdiction in different ways.

Fundamentally, there are three main duties in which a barrister regularly carries out:

- **Court appearances** – barristers often attend client court cases in order to represent them and act on their behalf;

> Barrister - "A person called to the Bar and entitled to practise as an advocate, particularly in the higher courts."
> (Oxford Dictionary, 2016)

- **Legal aid** – provide legal advice either face-to-face or through written documentation;
- **Draft court documents** – like many other job roles, the role of a barrister comes with a great deal of paperwork. Barristers will need to draft written documentations in order to use for court cases and tribunals.

THE INNS OF COURT

Any aspiring barrister who wishes to join the Bar, will need to join an Inn of Court. The Inns of Court offer a great deal of support to barristers and students. They act as a support system by offering educational activities, dining get-togethers, and various scholarships and grants.

Barristers work in Chambers as well as in-house and government departments. The Inns of Court are where most barristers train and eventually get 'Called to the Bar' (*see glossary for definition*). This is the process after graduating from completing the Bar Professional Training Course (BPTC). After the BPTC, you will need to obtain a pupillage and apply to an Inn of Court (*see glossary for definition*).

The Inns of Court include are:

- Grays Inn;
- Inner Temple;
- Lincoln Inn;
- Middle Temple.

These Inns are the only way in which a person can get *'Called to the Bar'*. Each of the aforementioned institutions have their own history and particular reasons for being well known in the professional circle of practising barristers. Therefore, it is up to you to consider which Inn you wish to join. Although they all offer similar services, they each have something unique to offer.

For more information on the Inns of Court, please visit the following website: www.barcouncil.org.uk.

IDENTIFYING BARRISTERS

At first glance, the role of a barrister looks pretty 'cool' compared to other legal professions. They can be identified as those in white wigs and black capes, striding about in courtrooms, pleading the cases of clients in front of a judge and jury.

The white wig and gown are synonymous with the exceptionally high standards of excellence and professionalism, paramount to the role of a good lawyer.

Regardless of whether you have seen them in court or on television, they are instantly recognisable because of these historical uniforms - steeped in hundreds of years of tradition and legal precedents.

THE ROLE OF A BARRISTER

In a generic sense, a barrister is a type of lawyer who is a Licensed Legal Practitioner (LLP), qualified to provide legal advice and support to the public.

Barristers will provide specialist legal aid for individuals and organisations in both court cases and tribunals. Foremost, they are usually hired by solicitors prior to the court case, in order to offer advocacy and support in the lead up to court proceedings.

In simpler terms, barristers are used to translate and make sense of a client's interpretation of events, and use the client's viewpoints in order to form a persuasive, legal argument. This argument will ultimately represent the client in the best manner, in hope to obtain the best outcome in court. For barristers, the best outcome is to simply try and win their case based on justification, interpretation and logical reasoning.

RESPONSIBILITIES AS A BARRISTER

Primarily, the role of a barrister is to provide in-depth, specialist, legal advice. They are based both in and out of court, offering support, knowledge and expertise to their clientele in hope to establish the truth and resolution.

A barrister is to act as an advocate for legal court cases. In simpler terms, they stand up in court, wear a wig and gown, and plead cases on their client's behalf.

Of course, the role of a barrister is more than simply wearing a wig and gown. They have an array of professional duties, and these all vary on a day-to-day basis.

Typical barrister duties include:

- Negotiating settlements;
- Drafting legal documents;
- Examining and cross-examining witnesses;
- Presenting arguments in court;
- Representing clients in court;
- Attending conferences with clients;
- Taking instructions from clients and solicitors;
- Preparing legal arguments;

- Writing opinions;
- Legal research;
- Understanding and interpreting law;
- Preparing cases for court.

The role of a barrister will vary depending on the *type* of barrister you wish to become. Barristers are able to specialise in different areas of the legal field, therefore providing more expertise in a particular area.

ESSENTIAL SKILLS AND QUALITIES

Before entering the profession you may consider whether you have the qualities needed to make it all the way in this profession.

<u>Some of these skills include:</u>

- I.T skills;
- Stamina;
- Integrity;
- Intellectual capabilities;
- Ability to digest large amounts of information in a short space of time;
- Presentation skills;
- Advocacy skills;
- Ability to stay calm under pressure;
- Good time and people management skills;
- Interpersonal skills.

Of course, the above list is not exhaustive of all of the qualities needed to become a barrister, but it does offer some of the most essential qualities in terms of a successful barrister.

DIFFERENCE BETWEEN BARRISTERS AND SOLICITORS

Before you progress in your pursuit in becoming a barrister, it is important that you know the difference between the role of a barrister and the role of a solicitor. There is sometimes confusion between the work carried out by the two, and you need to know the difference in order to know what profession you actually want.

It may seem obvious, but barristers and solicitors are NOT the same thing. Although there is an element of overlap between the two strands of the legal profession, they have their own distinct differences.

Below I have outlined some of the differences between the role of a barrister and the role of a solicitor.

- Solicitors are less likely to be in court than barristers. Barristers spend the majority of their time advocating in court.

This is especially more so for the higher courts such as the Crown Court for criminal cases and the High Court for civil matters, where solicitors require higher rights of audience.

- There have been some recent changes in the legal profession which allow for barristers to meet clients directly. Most of the work which barristers do is through the instructions of a solicitor.

You may need to consider if you prefer the work of a solicitor which involves spending more time with clients in the preparation of cases, such as through the taking of instructions for witness statements.

- Solicitors are generally the first port of call for clients. They are able to provide legal advice and support them through different situations. A barrister becomes important when cases are taken to court, and this is where they will stand up and represent the clients on their behalf.

- Qualification as a solicitor is upon successful completion of a law degree or graduate diploma in law followed by a 'Legal Practise Course' as opposed to a Bar Professional Training Course.

There is a requirement to complete two years of training as a 'trainee solicitor' and a personal skills course, rather than the one year (two times six months) 'pupillage' training that barristers must complete.

- A practising certificate is required every year upon admission to the Law Society from the Solicitors' Regulatory authority SRA rather than the Bar Standards Board.

Regulation of solicitors is by the SRA and their continued professional development (CPD) is required every year with a minimum of 16 hours education and training. Barristers are regulated by the Bar Standards Board and are required to complete 12 hours of CPD training.

- Solicitors collect information for cases such as expert evidence and reports. Barristers use this information in court to support their cases.

- Solicitors take statements from clients and barristers use these for the purpose of examination and cross-examination.

- Solicitors put together legal bundles for hearings and lengthy trials and barristers rely on these to prepare legal arguments for court cases.

- Solicitors are responsible for advising clients at police stations, courts and in solicitors' offices. Barristers have conferences with clients at Chambers or in court before hearings and trials.

- Solicitors are usually employed. Barristers mostly work for themselves with the exception of those working within companies or in government departments.

- Solicitors tend to specialise and spend their career working in one particular area such as crime or family. Barristers may take on a more varied case load.

Working as a barrister would allow you to make a direct difference in the lives of members of the public. In this way, you may consider the profession as being influential, similar to other professions such as teaching and medicine.

The profession is known to be vigorous and demanding and not everyone is cut out to be a barrister. This means careful thought needs to go into the decision of entering the legal world. The other thing to consider is that not everyone is able to make it through the full qualification process.

Though it is difficult, those who have both the ability and desire are able to succeed in their ambition to qualify as barristers; if not at the first attempt, then thereafter.

POTENTIAL EARNINGS

Though it is difficult to give precise figures for the potential earnings of qualified barristers, I can provide some rough guidelines. These may be helpful for those wanting to have a clearer idea on whether to enter the profession or what areas to specialise in.

Ultimately, as with most professions, becoming a barrister for purely financial gains would not allow you to have longevity in the profession. It is a tough and demanding profession, but one that requires passion and hard work.

> IMPORTANT TIP
>
> Make sure you understand the role of a barrister. You need to know how this role differs from other legal professions. Is the role of a barrister most suited to you? Do you have what it takes to make a successful career as a barrister? Ask yourself these questions when deciding whether this career is rightly for you.

Qualified barristers

Earnings of qualified barristers can vary, as widely as £25,000 to £300,000 a year, and is dependent on the following:

- Area of practice;
- Chambers;
- Level of promoting by clerks;
- Reputation;
- Personality;
- Location;
- Work load and holiday time;
- Junior barrister;
- Promotion to QC;
- Experience.

Area of work

On the whole, commercial work tends to be the most lucrative, and barristers can earn up to £200,000 a year from this type of work within the second year of practice. The figure may go down to £100,000 if focussing on areas such as family and crime.

Civil and public work may be somewhere in between these. Most barristers should expect to be earning around £100,000 by their second year of practice, regardless of which area they practice in.

Pupillages

In terms of pupillages, many Chambers may offer up to £60,000 to £65,000 for the year. However, some Chambers will offer considerably more. For example, Atkins Chambers currently offer £72,500 for pupillages in 2016, however this can be subject to change during the year.

> Please remember that, as they are mostly self-employed, barristers will also be liable to pay their own tax based on their incomes. This may considerably reduce the amount they bill over a year. These are in accordance with the Bar Standard Board regulations.

Queen's Counsel

In terms of QC, more commonly known as the Queen's Counsel, some QCs can demand millions of pounds on fees and there will be clients more than happy to pay for their services for their level of knowledge and experience. A lot of these QCs rely on reputation and past successes in order to be personally requested by clients.

> The minimum award for pupillages is £12,000, as set by the BSB, but most Chambers would offer much more than this.

You can check the Chambers Student Website for further details on salary.

WORKING HOURS

It is difficult to give a precise account of typical working hours of a barrister. Your working hours will vary on a day-to-day basis and this will often include long, unsociable hours.

You will often be required to work long evenings and weekends. This is particularly true at the start of your career, and therefore you should consider this when thinking of a career as a barrister.

OPPORTUNITIES FOR PROGRESSION

Once the pupillage has been completed, trainees can apply for tenancy and become junior barristers. Career progression depends on how much work you are willing to take on and how many hours you are prepared to put in.

The ultimate aim for most barristers is to take 'silk' and become a member of the QC. This requires taking the lead in serious cases or entering the judiciary as assistant reader before becoming a judge.

Other barristers may decide to enter the 'Employed Bar' and work for in-house departments of councils, in solicitors' firms, or in the public sector.

CHANGES IN THE PROFESSION

There have recently been some amendments to the way that barristers deal with clients. This means that they can now have direct access with clients, something preciously restricted in the past. There have also been changes to the funding by government funds for legal work, legal aid funding as well as the expansion for solicitors' rights of audience.

> Barristers' earnings will depend on the Chambers that they work in, and the area of work in which they specialise. For higher earning potential, commercial work tends to be the most lucrative.

- **Direct Access**

A fairly new change in the legal system is the introduction of direct access, or public access, which allows members of the public to approach barristers directly. Previously this was not allowed and individuals had to first go through a solicitor in order to use the services of a barrister. Now anyone needing legal advice or representation can bypass the need to contact a solicitor and just instruct a barrister directly. Not all barristers choose to undertake direct access work for a variety of reasons, but there are a growing number of individuals in the profession willing to offer this new service.

An advantage of this change includes saving costs for members of the public. It also increases the workload for barristers to take on new clients. Direct access also reduces unnecessary administrative time. The cost will just be for the work of the barrister, rather than both a solicitor and barrister, as well as court fees and additional expenses incurred.

Practical things such as agreement fees and payments from clients are now in the hands of barristers rather than solicitors. Barristers' clerks will deal with handling of client money. This probably is the biggest and most significant change to the barristers' profession.

<u>You are not allowed to do certain things for clients as a barrister acting under this scheme, such as:</u>

- Issuing proceedings in court on behalf of clients;
- Instruction of expert witnesses;
- Handling client money.

<u>Also, there are certain conditions on barristers being able to take on such cases including:</u>

- 3 years' experience practising as a barrister after completion of

training;
- Completion of the Public Access Training Course by the Bar Standards Board;
- Relevant notices, required by the Bar Code of Conduct.

It should be noted that not all cases are suitable for direct access, such as cases involving minors or legal aid. Direct access is best suited for straightforward cases.

• Solicitors' Increased Rights of Audience

Solicitors who have completed the relevant advocacy assessment are now offered 'higher rights of audience' which means that they can appear in the Crown Court and High Court. This has resulted in some cases not being given to barristers and dealt with in-house by solicitors within their own firms.

• Legal Aid and Fixed fees

Following government cuts in the legal aid budget, the decision was made by the Legal Services Commission to reduce the amount of funding for legal aid work. There has been a reduction in the amount of money available for certain cases and this has affected many areas in law, particularly in family law and criminal and civil work.

As clients are unable to afford to pay legal fees from their own pocket, it means that many cases are not going to court and as a knock-on effect, less income is being made for barristers from legal aid work.

Fixed fees have reduced the amount of hours that could precisely have been billed for legal aid work. Rather than charging for hourly rates for certain cases, travel, waiting and advocacy, barristers now have to agree to the fixed fee that would be paid upon completion of the case.

KEY POINTS

- The potential earnings of qualified barristers depend on the areas of work in which they practice.
- Chambers may pay between £12,000 and £70,000 for the pupillage stage of training.
- Other factors such as personality, experience and successful cases may affect potential earnings.
- QCs earn much more than normal barristers.
- Time spent on holiday and the number of hours worked have a large effect on barristers' earnings, as they are usually self-employed.
- Barristers need to be articulate and be able to work under pressure.
- Solicitors and barristers are different and despite some element of overlap in their work, barristers are likely to do more advocacy and a larger variety of legal work.
- The Chambers in which barristers practise are divided up into 4 Inns.
- Direct access means barristers can deal with clients directly without the need of solicitors.
- There are certain requirements of barristers to carry our direct access work.
- Legal aid cuts affect the amount of fees that barristers can charge for legal aid work.
- Many solicitors now have higher rights of audience in the Crown Court and High Court, which means they will not instruct barristers as previously required.

CHAPTER 2

AREAS OF WORK

Typical areas that you may wish to specialise can be categorised under the following headings:

- Criminal Law;
- Chancery Law (estates and trusts);
- Entertainment Law;
- Sports Law;
- Commercial Law;
- Common Law (family, housing and personal injury).

A further breakdown of the type of legal aid you can offer as a barrister includes:

Administrative and Public Law	Aviation	Banking	Chancery
Civil Law	Civil Liberties and Human Rights	Commercial Dispute Resolution	Common
Company Law	Competition	Construction	Crime
Employment	EU	Family	Immigration
Insolvency	Insurance	Intellectual Property	International Arbitration
Landlord and Tenant	Housing	Personal Injury	Planning
Professional Negligence	Property	Regulatory	Revenue Law
Shipping	Sports and Entertainment	Technology	Media

> Before you apply to become a barrister, you should have an idea of the area in which you want to work. As shown above, the role of a barrister will ultimately depend on which area you choose to specialise.

Below I have given a brief description of some of the main areas of work you can specialise in. Note, this list does not cover all of the different areas nor does it cover the areas in great detail, and so extended research may be required for in-depth information on each area of law.

Administrative & Public Law – This area of law provides services for a range of topics such as solar energy tariffs and the rights to die. Also covered would be areas such as the treatment of a disabled person by a local authority, or a child's right to an education. They advise local authorities or central government departments in areas of energy, transport and waste disposal.

Aviation & Aerospace – Provide regulatory, insurance and commercial advice and litigation services to the world's airlines, manufacturers and financiers. Aircraft finance and leasing are key areas of activity. Other issues that may be covered would include competition and state aid, emissions trading rules, insolvency and restructuring, and aviation disasters.

Banking & Finance – May act for the banks, carrying out due diligence on project contracts, as well as structure and formulate banks security packages on the off chance that something goes wrong. Some may advise borrowers themselves. Some may act for companies and sponsors that want to borrow from a bank to fund an infrastructure project.

Commercial Property & Real Estate – Act for a variety of clients; investors and developers, landowners, public sector bodies and governments. They will focus on buying, selling, letting and developing land. Planning, construction, litigation, environmental and tax law will commonly run side-by-side with real estate law. This area of law can operate across sectors such as corporate, investment, banking, health, education, insolvency, charities, agriculture and private wealth.

Construction & Engineering – Clients for this area include insurers, architects, industry associations, public authorities, governmental bodies for major corporations and partnerships and contractors. Work may include resolution of disputes by litigation, adjudication, mediation or arbitration. Drafting and negotiating contracts and advising on projects, health and safety, insurance, insolvency and environmental matters are some non-contentious work.

Crime – They deal with the full spectrum of offences - from murder all the way down to minor motoring misdemeanors. Barristers can act on the behalf of people who are guilty or not guilty.

Employment, Pensions & Incentives – Handle all areas of employment law. This would include workplace monitoring, staff restructuring, discrimination and whistle-blowing.

Family/Matrimonial – Advise on a wide range of legal issues relating to marriage, civil partnerships and unmarried couples. Separation, divorce, financial claims, pre and post-nuptial/civil partnership agreements and cohabitation. They will also help settle cases that involve children such as contact, support and adoption.

Housing (Landlord & Tenant) – Deal with cases ranging from terrorizing teens to bankrupt restaurateurs who owe rent or are unlawfully sub-letting. Also dealing with add-ons to a leased property such as a roof extension or a cellar. This area of law focuses a lot on the statutory obligations of public authorities to the poor or homeless.

Immigration – This area of practice deals with matters of immigration and nationality. Asylum, human rights, and immigration status for employees are also areas that would be covered.

Insolvency (Restructuring) –This deals with companies or organizations when they are unable to pay their debts and face liquidation. This work deals with advising organizations on how to avoid such situations and create contingency plans in case the worst happens.

Insurance (Reinsurance) – Responsible for advising their clients on investment management, coverage disputes, mergers and acquisitions of insurers, documentation, and the transfer of books and business between insurers.

Intellectual Property – Advise in two main areas: 'Hard' which relates to patents, registered designs and registered trademarks, and 'Soft' which relates to unregistered trademarks, database rights, trade secrets, copyright, unregistered design rights, confidential information and passing off.

Media & Entertainment – Clients in this area of practice include performers, managers, agents, creator's artistic work, owners of festival grounds and theatres, publishers and broadcasters, advertising agencies and distributors, and big brands who employ celebrities to endorse their products.

Shipping & Trade – Areas of practice within the shipping & trade section would be transport collisions, lending and security, charters and shipbuilding contracts.

Sports – This area involves legal issues in the world of both amateur and professional sports. It will overlap with employment law, contract law, competition law and tort, as well as intellectual property, privacy and defamation.

Technology, Media & Telecommunications – Advise on commercial and technical issues, regulatory changes, market developments, and legislation.

KEY POINTS

- Barristers' work is divided into different areas such as Chancery, Civil, Criminal and Common Law.
- There are many different strands of work underneath the aforementioned areas.
- Barristers can choose the areas that they are most interested in.
- The rewards for working in the different areas differ greatly financially.
- Criminal work may require much more contact with clients than commercial work.

CHAPTER 3

IS THE JOB RIGHT FOR ME?

Nobody can be 100% certain as to whether a career is right for them. You need to define yourself and your future based on what you think is right for you. You cannot base your life-important decisions based on what your family and friends want you to do; you need to make decisions based on what YOU want.

A career as a barrister should be thought about cautiously. The process is unbelievably demanding and requires extreme high levels of commitment and determination. This profession is not to be taken on light-heartedly.

The learning curve to any job does not stop as soon as you qualify. Your education, expertise and knowledge will constantly be tested during your time as a barrister. This process will likely to occupy you for many years beyond your initial training, so you need to be sure that this is what you really want to do.

It is imperative that you fully comprehend the requirements and the standards to which you will be held. As a barrister, you can expect a long-winded process that will require long hours, commitment and ambition to succeed.

This section is going to demonstrate both the upsides and downsides of the job role, and allow you to have a better idea as to whether or not you see yourself in this profession.

WHY CHOOSE TO WORK AS A BARRISTER?

There are many reasons why someone may choose a career as a barrister. If you enjoy public speaking, helping people, being challenged and thinking on your feet, then this could be an ideal path for you.

Before you decide whether this is an area in which you could work, consider the following:

- Are you articulate?
- Do you have a high standard of English language and education?
- Are you able to work under pressure?
- Can you read and analyse large amounts of information?
- Are you able to form clear, persuasive and logical arguments?

> Nobody ever knows if they are suitable for a particular career. Consider both the pros and cons of becoming a barrister, and weigh up whether you can see yourself in this long term career.

Barristers have an overriding duty to the court and administration of justice which means that they are always acting in the greater interest of society.

There are a lot of rewards for those who do decide to enter this profession and these include personal success in representing clients, recognition amongst peers and advancement to high profile cases with experience and determination.

Barristers are considered to be highly intelligent individuals who gain the respect of others for their ability to do a difficult job, both professionally and effectively. This is because there is a high standard of competence expected from them and they understand the need to maintain this standard in all that they do. If these challenges and rewards appeal to you, then becoming a barrister could be the right career choice.

Below I have outlined further reasons as to why you should become a barrister.

TOP REASONS TO BECOME A BARRISTER

The following reasons have been carefully put together to illustrate all of the positives and benefits of becoming a barrister.

1. Salary

Let's start with the most obvious one. One of the largest benefits that comes with the job role of being a lawyer is the salary. With starting salaries for your pupillage, you will work for a minimum of £12,000. This can be significantly higher depending on the Chambers and location in which you've applied.

Qualified barristers can earn anything between £25,000 and £300,000.

Barristers who have been in the legal game for over 10 years can earn a whopping £1,000,000 based on experience and expertise.

Another key thing to remember in regards to salary is that it is dependent on a number of factors. For example, salary is considered on the basis of experience, Chambers, location and the area of work in which you specialize.

> Unlike many other professions, you will start off on a reasonable salary. Your potential to earn more will solely depend on you. Generally, barristers are self-employed and therefore will need to find new clients and work hard, in order to keep earning.

2. Fulfilment

As a barrister, you will get the opportunity to make a difference in the lives of your clients on a daily basis. Not only can you make a difference with your clients, but you have the chance to make a difference in the lives of people everywhere. One case can set the precedence for many future cases, and therefore plays a vital role in the long-term legal process.

Having a job that allows you to feel attainment and gratification makes you realise that you have a worthwhile job which will allow you to feel a sense of accomplishment and success.

3. Advancement

After obtaining your degree and getting your license to practice law, you now have the opportunity to work your way up to the top and even become a judge in courts. Generally, you will be self-employed which means you have the opportunity to progress in your career at a speed that suits you. Becoming a barrister opens up a number of doors for future career prospects, which will ultimately inspire motivation and ambition for further success.

4. Education

Even if you don't go back to school for official advanced training, as a barrister you will constantly be learning. As a trainee you will have to undergo continuous training whilst working in order to make sure your knowledge is to a high standard.

Even long-term barristers still undergo training. While working on cases, you will be researching past cases as well as learning about obscure laws and differentiating jurisdictions.

There will always be learning opportunities for you to engage in, which will allow you to excel and broaden your horizons in terms of knowledge, expertise and experience.

5. Variety

Not only do you have a wide variety of specialised areas of practice to choose from, but your daily tasks will vary from day-to-day.

The job offers versatility as your work life will be changing constantly, making each day different.

Along your journey, you will meet an array of people, from other training barristers, to qualified barristers and judges, to new and existing clients. You will come across all walks of life in a range of different situations. No doubt this will bring variation to your working life.

6. Knowledge of the Law

Practising the law requires intellectual ability. Not only is your knowledge of the law essential to perform your job successfully, but it offers great benefits to your clients to ensure they are in capable hands of someone who is highly proficient and knowledgeable.

7. Great Career Prospects

A career in the legal industry offers interesting, competitive, stimulating prospects from beginning to end. Not a day goes by that you will find yourself bored. You are constantly on the go, and every day brings new challenges, new clients and new things to learn.

It really is a job like no other. Gaining satisfaction from knowing that you are making a difference is the best feeling, and you will continuously be feeling a sense of fulfilment and achievement.

8. Networking

As a trainee barrister, you will meet people from all different backgrounds. It is important to be able to engage in social activity and expand your profile, in order to 'get yourself out there'.

Whether that's interacting with other lawyers, gaining a new clientele base or simply offering your advice to friends and family, you will begin to notice that networking will help you build up a great professional and expanding portfolio of yourself as a qualified barrister.

It is true by saying that the more you network, the more chance you have of building a great and reputable portfolio of yourself.

THE DISADVANTAGES OF BECOMING A BARRISTER

As with any job, you will also have to consider the downsides of the job role.

I am not going to sugar coat it; becoming a barrister is extremely difficult. It is a demanding process, in more ways than one, and therefore you need to know what you are getting yourself into before continuing on with your legal journey.

1. Long Working Hours

12 hour days are not uncommon, especially during busy periods. Starting early and working late can happen frequently.

Weekend hours may be required on occasion and large city firms can work these extended hours on a regular basis. That means, work does not end as soon as you leave the office or courtroom. The on-going demands of the job requires you to put in the extra time and effort. 50 plus hour weeks are not uncommon for lawyers.

2. Lack of Work-Life Balance

The fact that you are required to '*take your job home with you*', as a matter of speaking, suggests the implications this can have on a person's work-life balance.

Many barristers complain about the difficulties of maintaining a healthy work and social life, and the impact this has on their personal life.

3. Law Debt

The cost of studying and training to become a lawyer is expensive. If you are not fortunate enough to get your tuition and maintenance paid for, you will need to get a loan of some sort. Therefore, once your studies have ended, you will be required to start paying off these loans.

4. Stress

This can be a very stressful position due to the long hours and workload and/or responsibilities.

There is a great deal of deadlines, responsibilities and client demands which are all factors of dealing with pressure, stress and time management.

5. Competitive Job Market

Increased competitive pressures have forced lawyers to settle with less than ideal circumstances regarding their career.

It is difficult enough to be a successful barrister, without the added pressure of competing for one job position, which is expected to receive over 20 applications.

6. Constantly Changing Legal Paradigms

The practice of law is continuously being challenged by other non-law sources. Lawyers no longer have the monopoly in regards to the law.

From self-help websites to the internet, legal advice and understandings can be instantly researched online. That means lawyers are losing work due to the available information online, therefore impacting the position in which they hold in the structure of the legal system.

CHAPTER 4

A BARRISTER'S PERSPECTIVE

Case Study "A barrister's perspective" – a qualitative study into the business and development of lawyers.

Within this chapter, I have provided you with an extensive one-to-one interview with a qualified barrister.

BACKGROUND INFORMATION

This interview was conducted with a well-established barrister at a London Chambers. The aim of this interview was to get an 'inside' look into the role of a barrister, and ask probing questions regarding the legal profession.

She has been a qualified barrister for over 16 years and worked on some high profile cases in various areas of law. I was fortunate enough to work with her, instructing her on many of my clients' criminal, asylum and human rights cases, over a period of 10 years. I worked with many barristers during my time as a solicitor, but her professional attitude and dedication to serving her clients was the reason that I sought her out for this chapter. My clients were always glowing with praise about her passion and ability to fight their case in court, even the most difficult cases. This level of commitment to her clients and all her years of experience means she is a well-established barrister.

She was kind enough to give answers to all of the questions I posed to her for this guide. I hope that you find this interview helpful in understanding more about the role of becoming a barrister.

INTERVIEW

Why did you decide to become a barrister?

'I always wanted to be a barrister from a young age, maybe as young as 7, and told my parents of my ambition. There were no barristers in the family and most of my family were in science-based professions such as medicine. I am not sure where the idea came from but it may have been from something I saw on television growing up. I really enjoyed English and Humanities when I was in school and studied English, History and Politics for A-levels. I enjoyed these subjects because I had a sensitive appreciation of people's feelings and emotions. From an early age I knew that I was a people's person – an integral quality for this profession. My dream to become a barrister was cemented once I got involved in debates at school and realised that I not only had a flair for it, but also really enjoyed it.'

What was your experience of studying law at university?

'I went to UCL in London to study for my law degree and the Bar was already on my mind. There was a courtroom at UCL and also a moot room with benches. I got heavily involved in mooting and regularly entered competitions. These were mostly internal competitions and I became very successful in them, reaching the final in my first year of competing. I was also an active member of the student's branch of the Law Society. I also became moot secretary of the university's Law Society which meant running the moots, and then in

my second year of university, judging them. I was also heavily involved in the Debating Society and it was great practice for both my speaking and debating skills. All in all, I gained an amazing range of experiences during my three years at university and it was the best grounding for my legal career.'

Are there any particular subjects that you would recommend for law students interested in becoming barristers?

'I did half of my finals in the second year of my degree and the other half in my third year. I would suggest that students interested in the Bar should take options like Evidence, Jurisprudence, Law and Literature, Media and Entertainment. These provide a good knowledge of basic legal procedures and also help with specialisms later on. Criminal law is usually mandatory but crucial because as a pupil, many of your briefs will be criminal cases and your 'bread and butter' for a year or so. It is important to get a good understanding of this area and work hard to secure good marks.'

Are there any non-academic activities you would suggest whilst at university to help enter the Bar?

'I would really recommend that undergraduates go to as many networking events as possible in order to forge relationships. Universities usually organise these at regular periods of the academic year and it is a good idea to get the dates to attend. I met many judges, solicitors, barristers and other legal professionals at these events and the conversations were invaluable. The professionals come from all different backgrounds and age groups meaning

they have very different and real working knowledge to share.'

What else gave you an advantage when it came to applying for the Bar?

'After completing my law degree at UCL, I went to study an MPhil in Criminology at Cambridge University. I had the option to study Sociology and Psychology whilst I was there, and this really helped broaden my understanding of human emotions and related issues. I was also able to take part in the university Law Society and Debating Society, as well as further my networking. You need to be well rounded in both academia and extra activities. I also did 8 research papers and a thesis on the effects of cannabis on individuals and whether the classification was suitable in light of these. I did it out of personal interest in the subject area, but it really assisted me later on in my application process as I had a lot to talk about at the interview stage.'

What does the training involve to become a barrister?

'After completing the law degree (LLB), or conversion course (CPE) if you have a non-law degree, you need to apply to do the Bar Professional Training Course (BPTC) at a qualifying Bar School. You need a first class degree or at least a 2:1 classification to get into a good training school. It helps to have a good CV at this point with various relevant experiences and activities, especially at the interview (see Creating Your CV for details). Once you successfully complete your BPTC, you need to apply for a pupillage. This can be very competitive, so I would suggest doing something to make yourself stand out. I am now often involved in selecting candidates and in a mountain of applications and CVs,

we are looking for something in a candidate that is different.'

What are the pros and cons of the job?

'The good thing about this job is that you are self-employed at the Inns of Bar which means that you can have a degree of flexibility with your time and workload. It is a really interesting profession which is both academically and practically demanding. As the law is always changing you can never really master it, but it helps to keep the job fresh and exciting. You are dealing with real people and real problems, and therefore you need to always be challenging yourself to become a better advocate. There is no day that is ever the same in this job and you never know what an opponent or witness will say. It's a very exciting job with a lot of adrenalin running through you every time you are in court. This is what I love the most – the buzz I get from the unknown and uncertainty. There is a good mixture of academia and practical law and I am always thinking about how to interpret it. What I love is that there is always scope for legal argument within the grey area. However, the best thing about this job is that you can help people who are vulnerable and fight for them. When you get a good result for them it is a really satisfying feeling. With good advocacy you can turn a case around, even the more difficult ones.

You will notice that all barristers have their own style and you will have to work out what your style or approach is. With witnesses, you never quite know what their mind-set is, so you have to be clever to get what you want. At all times you have to be flexible and willing to think on your feet. A good command of the English Language and of vocabulary is required. Many barristers combine their advocacy with other work such as lecturing, writing academic articles, mooting, helping juniors and spin-off careers such as mediators. I know some barristers that have become expert witnesses and part time judges in or out of jurisdiction.

One of the other things I love about this profession is that there is a very active social life and a lot of comradery. You get to go out with clerks and colleagues after your work is finished and there is healthy competition between colleagues for work. Once the clerks know that you are very competent with legal argument and willing to work hard, they will give you commercial arrangements between then and solicitors. We are able to use the facilities of the Inns of Court such as the lunches and dinners. It is an old and ancient institution with privilege and honour.

The cons of the job are that it can utterly consume you. Papers can be late, there is always work to be done and you can never be on top of it all. The work is literally never ending at times with many evenings and weekends being taken up by extra preparation. You need a really understanding family as this is not a regular nine to five job. It is really important to look after your mental and physical health. It can be particularly physically arduous if you are doing criminal work as there is a lot of travelling involved with a trolley of papers. It can be very stressful in court at times. It is not a job for those who are afraid of confrontation. Though it is usually civilised in court, you still need to be able to put up a good fight and make your voice heard. You sometimes need to be able to argue that black is white, and disagree with others if the situation requires.

There are instances where you may not like a client on a personal level, such as a paedophile and there are many cases where you have to read through very distressing information and facts. You need to be able to overlook this, and undergo your job in a professional and non-discriminatory manner.

Before this you have to rely a lot on your clerk for work. There is no set salary and sometimes financially you have to wait to be paid such as with legal aid work. You have to do your own bookkeeping and administration so you need to learn double entry bookkeeping so you don't rely on clerks. This is important because the clerks can make mistakes. You have to keep an eye on accounts. There is a very popular and true saying in this profession that you are 'only as good as the last case you did' and therefore you can never drop your standards, whether you like your client or not.

The bigger and more prestigious work comes later on and making money is not a good reason to join the profession. It was hard to find a pupillage before but not so much now. Clerks are the engine room of the barrister's Chambers and have their own hierarchy. It is important to get on with clerks to make sure you get work. The other down side of being a barrister is that there is often a lot of last minute work. You have to be prepared to cancel social plans if need be. You need to be available for work and ready to offer your services when required and called upon. There is a need to assimilate a huge amount of information, maybe 500 pages, in an evening and then spot the key/relevant points to distil legal argument for the following days. Organising your time and trying to create a healthy work-life balance can seem impossible at times.'

How much can you realistically earn as a barrister?

'Commercial barristers will earn at least £40,000, even as pupils, if in the best Chambers. However, they will earn less for criminal and family work. You will also find that legal aid work is less well paid. However, big jury trials for criminal cases do often pay well. In family law, ancillary relief work is well paid. You can earn between £35,000 and £100,000 for family work. If you are doing mainly private immigration work, then you can earn between £45,000 and £100,000 a year. Commercial work is better paid than other areas and top QC's often earn over a million pounds a year. Junior barristers doing immigration work will get at least £50,000 a year.

You have to take into account some costs which barristers incur. These include the Chambers rent which will most likely be around £450 a month. This has to be paid on time every month to keep your place in the Chambers. There is also clerking commission which is around 12% of receipts. Then there is also tax, VAT and travel costs to consider, too.'

Can you describe a typical working day?

'There isn't one because you can end up working all the time. You definitely need holidays though as there is a risk of overworking. With court hearings, if they are far away, then you need to be up earlier to get there on time especially to meet clients. There is a lot of travel involved in my area of work. I would usually wake up at 6am on a weekday and latest at 7am. I can go into Chambers at any time of the day. If I have a hearing, then I can meet the client in the morning for a conference. There is potentially a lot of waiting in court. Also I would deal with a lot of work emails and administrative tasks. I write up cases for solicitors almost on a daily basis and try to do this straightaway.

I like to call the solicitors firm who have instructed me on the case and tell them the result of the case as soon as possible. I would also call the Chambers clerk so that I may get some extra work that day. So the day may involve going to court in the morning, then writing up the case and finally prepping for the next day. There is no set pattern for a typical working day as a barrister. You have to be able to adapt to the constant changes.'

What makes a really good barrister?

'You need to be a really good thinker, listener and also a good talker. You should be emotionally intuitive both academically and mentally. A top barrister would be flexible with their approach to others and be able to think on their feet. Confidence is a must as well as good presentation skills and an ability to be persuasive. Of course, early on in your career, you need to demonstrate that you are intelligent and motivated.

A really good criminal barrister would be good on their feet whereas a chancery barrister who deals with trusts and wills, would need to be more academic. No matter what area of work you specialise in, you must be a people's person. You are not just a barrister, but a social worker, a friend and a counsellor. You need to get on with people from all walks of life without judging them, and bond with people within minutes of meeting them e.g. meeting them before court and gaining their trust. I think you are basically fulfilling many different functions; functions that all make up a successful lawyer.

You have a duty to your instructing solicitors and a duty to court. Although there is potential for these roles to conflict, you will remain professional and effective. Overall you must be an ethical person. The best barristers have a full package of skills, and both a flair and practical application for advocacy. Conviction, determination and a huge work ethic are also essential. As it is a really tough and demanding career, strength of character is important. The best barristers are brave and willing to fight for somebody in court, yet still remaining caring and empathetic in conferences with their clients.

I would say overall that you must be really dedicated and make this work a way of life because it is not just a job, but a lifestyle choice. It is definitely not for those who don't like hard work.'

Once qualified, what's the best way to gain experience?

'At a minimum, you need to have two pupillages at six months each. Then you will be taken on as a pupil barrister. The next stage is junior barrister and finally after sufficient experience and successful application, silk. When completing your pupillage, you will work on cases belonging to a qualified barrister, but you will be given some responsibility in that case, and then be able to take on your own cases, too. Those who are qualified should try to work at a general common law Chambers where they can gain experience in areas such as family, housing, criminal and immigration law. These are best for developing advocacy skills and to become robust as you will visit prisons and go before juries. Attending bail hearings for immigration and criminal cases is also very good experience.

When you are a junior you should really get some experience with injunctions, in particular non-molestation orders for family cases. Further invaluable experience would be obtained in doing criminal cases by prosecuting and defending. The top ten percent of barristers take silk and you have to apply to be considered. Ten years is the minimum length of experience before you may be considered. This title is the benchmark of quality and upon obtaining this, you can no longer take bread and butter cases but the more high quality and paid work. It is possible to take silk and still be a barrister or a judge, or alternatively not be silk and still become a judge.'

What does the training involve and what are the best courses and universities?

'You must have an initial law degree, an LLB or conversion course such as the CPE, and then complete the BPTC. This course is studied at Bar School and you need to have a 1st or 2:1 degree to get into a good quality school. You need to stand out in other ways too such as speaking other languages and have hands-on experience, mini-pupillages and marshalling experience.

After this you need to apply for a pupillage and this is two sets at six months each. It can be longer than two and you could do a third or fourth set with Chambers, too. Once completed you can get tenancy meaning that you are a full member of Chambers. You will be offered this by the Chambers that you do the pupillage with or possibly somewhere different.

Where you apply depends on the type of work that you want to do. For media work or immigration work, London is the best place to be. For family and crime, any big city is suitable. Commercial Law can be practised in London or Birmingham.'

Who are the governing bodies for barristers?

'The Bar Council, now the Bar Standards Board, is the governing body for barristers. They handle all the issues concerned with training and as a barrister, you have to pay annual fees to them. They also regulate discipline and handle complaints. CPD (continuing professional development), is a requirement and all barristers must complete 12 hours every year. However in the first three years of qualifying as a barrister this requirement is 42 hours. All barristers must have a practising certificate every year from the BSB. Barristers need to register separately with the Information Commissioner. Finally, you also need to be up to date on the barristers list and have professional indemnity insurance. (For more information, see the chapter Regulation and Continued Professional Development).'

What tips would you give for anyone wanting to train and work as a barrister?

'I would suggest that you go and sit in the public gallery of the local Magistrates and Crown Court. You should go to watch hearings at tribunals for immigration and employment cases. You can tell the ushers at these courts that you are a member of the public who would like to see some cases being heard and they will allow you to enter the rooms. You can then see how it is done and get a fascinating insight into the profession before beginning your career as a barrister.

I would also recommend you watch and read 'Rumpole of the Bailey' and

'Silk' as they both are high quality programmes about the life of barristers, and are also quite accurate. I suggest reading newspapers about cases in the U.K and overseas as they could ask about these cases at interviews for pupillage. You may need to argue one way or another about these, so you need to show that you have taken an interest in current and past legal cases.

At school I think it's a good idea to get involved in debating so you develop the relevant skills for advocacy early. Also you should take part in mooting at university and go to solicitors offices for work experience. Being an outdoor clerk and shadowing barristers is very beneficial too. Mini-pupillages will assist with securing places at Bar School later. It will also look good on your CV. Having a high quality and relevant CV is crucial to success in obtaining a place at the Chambers of your choice.'

KEY POINTS

- The profession can be very demanding both physically and mentally.
- There is scope to practise in different areas.
- Being a barrister is a rewarding profession as you can make a real difference in people's lives.
- You are able to combine other areas of related work with being a barrister.
- You need to be responsible for your time as you are working on a self-employed basis.

CHAPTER 5

ENTRY REQUIREMENTS

There are three stages of training in order to become a barrister in the UK. These include:

1. **Academic Qualifications**
2. **Vocational Training**
3. **Pupillage**

I will go into extensive detail about each of the aforementioned stages.

ACADEMIC QUALIFICATIONS

The first stage of training for the Bar is referred to as the **academic stage** and this requires the completion of a qualifying law degree.

SCHOOL AND COLLEGE

Although there is no real requirement in the types of A-Levels you choose, you should try to obtain A-Levels in subjects that can help you in a legal career. You may have to explain your choice of subjects and how they would assist your degree.

For example, if you took an A-Level in Art, you could state how this has prepared you to look at things from different perspectives and demonstrate your abilities to think both strategically and artistically.

Another example is Maths. If you obtained an A-Level in Maths, this demonstrates key skills such as critical understanding, thinking strategically, analyse and interpret data and information, and problem solving.

THE LAW DEGREE ROUTE

Qualifying with a law degree is probably the most straightforward way to become a barrister. Your studies will include all the required aspects of your academic training; essential for any aspiring lawyer.

The foundation subjects are:

i) **Public Law** (including Constitutional Law, Administrative Law and Human Rights)
ii) **Law of the European Union**
iii) **Criminal Law**
iv) **Obligations** (including Contract, Restitution and Tort)
v) **Property Law**
vi) **Equity and the Law of Trusts**

Alongside the above subjects, you will also be required to have knowledge in the following:

- Legal Research Skills;
- English Legal System;
- A chosen area of Legal Study.

THE NON-LAW DEGREE ROUTE

The non-law degree route, commonly referred to as the conversion route, is another way in which you can train to become a barrister.

If you have an undergraduate degree in another subject such as English or Biology and wish to enter the Bar, then you will need to pass the Common Professional Examination (CPE), also known as the Graduate Diploma in Law (GDL).

This conversion course may be sufficient if it has been approved by the regulatory body. These are both postgraduate qualifications and the Central Applications Board is the place to apply for enrolment on either of these courses.

Before this you may need to check with the Bar Standards Board whether your qualifications are approved or sufficient to satisfy the academic stage of the process. There may be a possibility to study these diplomas part time if provided by the institution.

As mentioned in the law degree route, there are certain subject areas which will need to be covered before moving onto the vocational stage of training:

i) **Public Law** (including Constitutional Law, Administrative Law and Human Rights)

ii) **Law of the European Union**
iii) **Criminal Law**
iv) **Obligations** (including Contract, Restitution and Tort)
v) **Property Law**
vi) **Equity and the Law of Trusts**

Entering the CPE/GDL qualification should be considered carefully as they are expensive and you may not be able to obtain a refund on your fees if you decide to drop out midway through the course. A full and serious commitment is essential in order to complete either of these.

IMPORTANCE OF ACADEMICS

It is the aim of this academic part of the training to make sure that all students are sufficiently equipped with the requisite level of academic theory and knowledge from which they can build on to complete the vocational training. The vocational training is the Bar Professional Training Course (BPTC).

COMMON PROFESSIONAL EXAMINATION (CPE) (At a higher education provider or legal institution recognised by the Central Applications Board). **Graduate Diploma in Law with a recognised institution.**

The BPTC is fundamentally a course which has been designed to complement barrister's training in order to make them more competent and effective in their profession. The course equips students with the essential skills and knowledge to obtain a pupillage; the final stage of training.

SECURING YOUR DEGREE

Although it is more beneficial for those who have completed the academic stage to have achieved high degree classifications, anything up to a 2:2 UK Honours degree would be acceptable to most providers.

It should be noted that even if accepted onto the vocational stage, it is unlikely that an individual with a 2:2 would be able to obtain a pupillage which is the next stage of the training process for barristers.

KEY POINTS

- The academic stage involves obtaining a qualifying law degree such as an LLB.
- A non-law degree accompanied by a CPE or GDL is sufficient to satisfy the academic stage.
- A good classification is required to successfully obtain a place at the vocational stage of training.
- There are certain core subjects which need to be studied at university or law school to obtain a qualifying law degree.

VOCATIONAL TRAINING

The Bar Professional Training Course (BPTC) is the vocational stage of the qualification process for becoming a barrister. This was previously known as the Bar Vocational Course (BVC) and only recently changed to accommodate some changes in 2010-11. To apply for this part of the training, you first need to apply online through the application system called BarSAS. A £50 payment must be made for this application process and the payment is non-refundable.

According to the Bar Standards Board every year there are around 2,500 applications for just 2,164 places on the BPTC. This means that competition is quite fierce to get onto the course and applications must be strong. It is possible to do the BPTC over one year full time or two years part time. By following the course part time you could also carry out some paid work and gain some legal experience.

THE PURPOSE OF THE BPTC

The purpose of the BPTC is to prepare students with the skills needed for a career at the Bar. It has advocacy, role play and drafting legal documents as the core components of the course. There are also other important aspects such as writing opinion; a skill which has to be frequently used as a practising barrister.

<u>Before students can start the BPTC they must fulfil the following requirements:</u>

1. **Successfully passing the Bar Course Aptitude Test (BCAT)**
(The next chapter will go into extensive detail about the BCAT and provide some example questions of what you can expect in this assessment).

2. **Fluency in English**
(Whether English is your first language, you will need to be fluent in English. You need to be able to articulate yourself both verbally and in written communication. For further details, please visit the Bar Standards Board website.)

3. **Joining an Inn of Court**
(You need to apply for an Inn of Court if you wish to be Called to the Bar).

However students are allowed to apply for the BPTC before they have completed the BCAT. The BCAT is primarily designed to test two things:

- Students' ability to think critically;
- Students' reasoning skills.

The above skills are crucial to the BPTC and are good indicators of how students will fare in the vocational training before making the commitment to undertake the course. This test was only a recent addition as a pre-requisite to the BPTC in 2012. It is possible to practice questions similar to those in the actual BCAT by going to the Pearson Vue website which can be found as a link on the Bar Standards Board website.

Once students feel ready to undertake the actual BCAT then they can register and schedule their test on the Pearson Vue website.

In the last chapter, *helpful resources*, there is a list of current recognised providers for the BPTC with details of how to contact them by both email and telephone.

COSTS FOR THE BPTC

The fees for following the BPTC are quite high but also vary depending on individual providers. Students can contact each provider directly for details of fees and payment options. Most providers include all course materials and books with their fees but you should check before making a commitment to pay.

According to the Bar Standards Board for 2015/16, the fees range from £12,500 all the way up to £18,000. These figures include all fees and deposits and each provider will ask for a non-refundable deposit to be paid by students once they have been accepted onto a course.

Taking this into consideration, students wishing to pursue the vocational stage of the training should make provisions for paying these fees.

<u>Options which could be explored to fund the course include:</u>

- Taking a loan from a Bank or Building society. Many have loans specific for vocational training courses and may offer a preferential rate of interest to ordinary loans for other purposes;

- Applying for an Inns scholarship (this must be done by the November of the year the course is due to start);

- Obtaining an award from Chambers. This could vary in amount and many include an advance from the pupil stage;

- Borrowing money from family members or business owners which may not need to be paid back immediately and won't incur the interest a bank loan would;

- Working alongside the BPTC, if being undertake as part time. There is likely to be no time to work if studying the BPTC full time;

- Obtaining a scholarship from the individual provider.

The fees for the BPTC are not cheap, currently ranging from £12,500 up to £18,000. It is important to arrange finance for this stage of training in order to have the ability to pay for the course upon acceptance.

OVERSEAS STUDENTS

For overseas students there is no barrier to applying for a place on the BPTC, but the fees charged may vary from those for home and EU students.

Also, there is no guarantee that achieving the vocational qualification will lead to entitlement to practice as a barrister in England and Wales. This is dependent on immigration status and a person's eligibility to work in the UK.

For a student overseas wanting to take the course, it would be best to check eligibility criteria and contact the providers directly.

For pupils in which English is not their first language, you need to meet the following requirements:

- You will also be required to have fluency in English and this means if you are a non-native speaker from overseas, then you will need a minimum of a 7.5 in all parts of the IELTS test;

- The alternative English qualification acceptable is a score of at least 73 in the Pearson English academic test.

BPTC MODULES

So once you are accepted onto the BPTC, here are some of the modules that you are likely to study, some compulsory and others optional:

Compulsory subjects

Advocacy	Conference	Opinion Writing	Drafting
Criminal Litigation and Evidence	Civil Litigation and Evidence	Professional Ethics	Resolution of Disputes outside of Court

Optional subjects

Advanced Criminal Litigation	Advanced Civil Litigation	Employment	Judicial Review	International Trade
Intellectual Property	Property and Chancery	Company Law	Family Law	Asylum and Detention

It should be noted that each provider will have their own way of teaching and a number of optional modules available to study.

Students should start thinking about areas of interest before they start the course in order to assist in choosing from the optional subjects available.

<u>Additional benefits that may be provided during the course could include:</u>

- Pro bono work;
- Working together in small groups;
- Mock trials and mooting judged by members of the judiciary;
- Court visits.

WHAT THE BPTC CONSISTS OF

All BPTC students are required to complete the following standardised exams on the same day at the same time, regardless of which institution they are undertaking their course.

They are a combination of multiple choice questions (MCQ's) and short answer questions (SAQ's):

- **Professional Ethics** - 2 hours; 20 MCQ's and 3 SAQ's
- **Criminal Litigation** - Evidence and Remedies; 3 hours 40 MCQ's and 5 SAQ's
- **Criminal Litigation** - Evidence and Sentencing; 3 hours 40 MCQ's and 5 SAQ's

A minimum mark of 60% is required to pass each of these tests, but there is an opportunity to re-sit them at a later day if unsuccessful at the first attempt.

KEY POINTS

- The Bar Professional Training Course (BPTC) is the vocational stage of barristers' training.
- You must apply to an approved BPTC provider for a place.
- Funding and scholarships may be available to assist with fees for the course.
- The BPTC can be studied one year full time or over two years part time.
- There are compulsory and optional subjects that have to be studied to obtain the BPTC.
- There are standard exams which are completed by all BPTC students at the same time.
- Overseas students will need to check they can legally work as barristers in the UK, even after qualification.

PUPILLAGE

Once students have completed both the academic and vocational stage of training, there is just one final hurdle left on the journey to becoming a barrister. This final stage is called the **pupillage** and it must be completed within five years of completing the BPTC.

A Chambers or Authorised Training Organisation (ATO) may offer a pupillage to any suitable student upon application. However, any provider must meet the requirements of Bar Training Regulations which govern pupillages.

If not satisfactory, then the pupillage may not be valid to qualify as a barrister. The application for a pupillage needs to be made directly to the Chambers or ATO. Consideration should be given to the volume of applications that are received for pupillages.

The length of the pupillage is twelve months in total and is usually broken up into two parts:

- '**First six**' which is the 'non-practising' part under the supervision of a pupil supervisor. During this period the pupil can only carry out supervised work. This could include assisting in writing opinion or drafting documents for court cases.

- '**Second six**' which is the period for the pupil to carry out their own work which is still supervised but which they can now be paid for.

The pupillage would normally start in the September or October of the year following acceptance. Some ATO's may consider different start dates and these would need to be arranged with the provider.

There is a minimum payment of £12,000 which has to be awarded for the pupillage. However most Chambers and ATO's give substantially greater awards. These can be as much as £65-70,000 for the 12 months at the highest paying Chambers.

Obtaining a pupillage is often seen as the hurdle which separates those who successfully go on to complete their training to become barristers and those who change their path to do something different instead. Successfully qualifying as a barrister is a highly applaudable achievement, given the level of competition and commitment required.

It is best to apply early for a pupillage and to apply to one of the higher paying Chambers. This could mean the difference between being paid the minimum of £12,000 for the 12 months of training, or £60,000.

KEY POINTS

- The pupillage is obtained by successfully applying to a barristers' Chambers or an authorised training organisation ATO.
- The pupillage is the final stage of training to qualify as a barrister.
- There are two six month periods for the 12 months to be completed called the first six and second six.
- Pupillages usually start in September or October of the year following acceptance.
- Pupils are awarded a minimum of £12,000 for the years training but this is usually much higher.

CHAPTER 6

REGULATION AND CONTINUED PROFESSIONAL DEVELOPMENT

Once you have finally qualified as a barrister having completed all academic, vocational training and pupillage, there are still certain regulatory requirements remaining.

There have been some recent changes to the regulation of the profession and the Bar Standards Board is responsible for the regulation of barristers, including dealing with complaints against individual barristers.

Included in this brief chapter are some details of the regulatory requirements for barristers to abide by.

PRACTISING CERTIFICATE

Firstly, all practising barristers must have an annual practising certificate. This can be renewed online by completing the Authorisation to practise section and paying practising certificate fees.

(PCF) Renewal is through an online system called Barrister Connect. In this system you must provide certain information which includes:

- Verifying contact details;
- Verifying practising status;
- Confirm CPD;
- Indemnity insurance;
- Paying the fee;
- Signing a declaration of truth.

The fee that is payable depends on the income band of the individual barrister. The fees increase incrementally with income.

As a guideline, for the year 2016-17 barristers earning between £30,000 and £60,000 must pay £220 for the year. Anything between £60,001 and £90,000 is £441 and then there is a large increase for those earning above £90,000 as the fees go up to £803.

There is a slight increase in fees year on year and these changes can be found on the Bar Standard Board website.

CONTINUED PROFESSIONAL DEVELOPMENT

This is an important aspect of ongoing training and education for barristers and is supervised by the Bar Standards Board (BSB). Spot checks are made at random to ensure that barristers have actually complied with CPD requirements since May 2014. Therefore barristers must keep records of all CPD training they have received with evidence such as certificates of attendance.

The courses which are recognised by the Bar Standards Board for CPD purposes are usually found listed on the BSB website. If barristers have individual enquiries regarding CPD training and recognised providers, then they can check with the BSB by sending an email to CPDrecords@barstandardsboard.org.uk.

There are different CPD requirements depending on the practising year of the individual barrister, but as a guide there are two programmes:

1) Now Practitioners Programme (NPP)

All barristers in their first three years of practise must do a minimum of 45 hours CPD and out of this, a minimum of 9 hours must be advocacy training, 3 hours ethics and 33 hours CPD. All CPD must be with providers recognised and accredited by the BSB.

2) Established Practitioners' Programme (EPP)

This is for those barristers who have been in practice for at least 3 years. The CPD courses are all over the country and are even available overseas as well as online.

There is provision for those unable to afford the full fees, but a minimum of 12 hours CPD is required each calendar year for barristers. Out of this, 4 hours must be accredited by the Bar Standards Board. A fee of £45 is payable by practitioners for those who wish to apply for consideration of one off accreditation by the BSB.

THE BARRISTER'S REGISTER

All barristers are required to fill their details on this online database which contains information on all practising barristers in England and Wales. It includes discipline information and the practising status of all individual barristers as well as the practising address.

KEY POINTS

- Once qualified, barristers need to have a practising certificate every year.
- CPD is required for all qualified barristers.
- In the first three years of practise, barristers must complete 45 hours of CPD every calendar year.
- After three years of practise barristers must compete 12 hours of CPD every calendar year.
- CPD courses must be approved by the Bar Standards Board.
- All barristers are required to register their details on an online database called The Barrister's Register.

CHAPTER 7

BAR COURSE APTITUDE TEST (BCAT)

Those seeking entry to the Bar Professional Training Course (BPTC) will need to undergo the Bar Course Aptitude Test (BCAT).

The Bar Course Aptitude Test (BCAT) is the first step of a candidate's training for becoming a barrister. The BCAT is a form of psychometric testing which assesses a person's level of performance regarding the legal sector.

Since 2013, the test has been made compulsory, thus, anyone wishing to undertake a Bar Professional Training Course (BPTC), needs to pass the Bar Course Aptitude Test. The test is created to ensure that only the candidates with the potential to pass the BPTC undertake the assessment.

Although passing this test does not necessarily guarantee that you'll make a good barrister, it can however give some indication as to whether or not you may be cut out for the position.

Based on the Watson-Glaser critical thinking appraisal, the BCAT is a useful tool to measure a candidate's abilities required for aspiring barristers. It is a test that aims to explore a person's intellectual and cognitive skills, both in terms of logical and critical understandings.

HOW IS THE BCAT MEASURED?

The BCAT is used to measure candidate's critical thinking and reasoning skills in order to demonstrate their suitability for the job role.

Becoming a barrister is a challenging process. These tests are specifically designed so that candidates 'think on their feet',. They need to be able to think outside of the box, and take every possibility into consideration. Thus, this test will primarily deal with assessing a candidates suitability and measure their competencies and skills required to become a barrister.

WHAT IS CRITICAL THINKING?

Critical thinking can be defined as 'thinking logically – using an objective approach to evaluate arguments and using relevant information to draw conclusions.' An integral part of the role of a barrister is to handle different situations and be able to engage in different understandings and perspectives in order to form a logical understanding of events.

The term 'critical thinking' can be structured through an organised framework which helps to facilitate high levels of knowledge and awareness. The "**RED MODEL**" is a way of breaking down the most important and valuable elements of the critical thinking process, in order to provide an in-depth account of a situation with truth, accuracy and integrity.

THE "RED MODEL"

Here is a table displaying the "RED MODEL" and the important skills required for any aspiring barrister:

Recognising Assumptions	Evaluate Arguments	Draw Conclusions
• Identifying assumptions is an important element for any aspiring Barrister. • It is **deceptive to assume** that the information you are given is completely factual • You need to consider every inch of the **evidence** and justify its logic and validity. • Identifying and questioning the difference between **truth** and **assumption** is imperative. • Such unfound logic and **uncertainty** helps reveal missing aspects of the **truth**. • Looking at things from different angles is a useful way to **analyse** indefinite circumstances.	• **Evaluating** arguments entails objective and accurate analysis. • Being able to identify weak **arguments** and gaps in missing **evidence** is crucial. • Questioning the **strength** of an argument and understanding **mitigating circumstances** is a vital skill to the role. • The job requires a person to remain **objective**. They cannot be seen to get emotionally attached or share their viewpoints. • They act as an **impartial** judge who subsequently tries to gather up as much information as possible.	• Piecing together all of the information, **evidence** and facts to arrive at a **conclusion** is the most important part of the process. • The **logic** of the decision must be accountable through **evidence** and **justification**. • Candidates who are able to show no generalisations in the process and are able to change their view if required. They are candidates who are described as having "**good judgement**". • The art of any candidate being able to show levels of **integrity**, **will-power** and **determination** will help to find the best possible conclusion.

The "**Red Model**" can be used as a guideline in order for you to complete the BCAT. These are typical steps that you could follow when assessing arguments, conclusions and assumptions.

The BCAT requires you to think logically. In order for you to do this, you have to think carefully about everything you read and everything you are told. You need to be able to recognise if the proposed argument or conclusion is accurate and whether or not it can be justified. Can the conclusion or assumption be reached by what you have been told? Is there any significant information missing which is needed in order to make that final conclusion?

Remember, this test is based on facts. You cannot answer these questions based on personal views or what you believe to be the truth. You have to take each question at face value, and remember, you can only come to a conclusion based on what you've read, not what you think!

WHAT TO EXPECT

The BCAT format uses statements and conclusions; of which the candidate must answer in a particular way depending on the type of question they are answering. The test consists of 5 basic question types, all of which will appear on your real BCAT. Each question type is used in order to assess a particular skill or ability that is required in the role of a barrister. The five question types are as follows:

Inference	A conclusion that can be drawn from facts or supposed facts.
Recognition of Assumptions	Something that is presupposed or anticipated. Something that is often taken for granted.
Deduction	The ability to come to a conclusion based on the information you are provided with.

Interpretation	How you interpret and understand the statement, in order to form a conclusion.
Evaluation of Arguments	Measuring an arguments strengths and weaknesses to determine how well it forms a solid argument.

In the real BCAT, you will be provided with these 5 testing questions. For each question, you will decide what answer appears most appropriate. Your score will depend on the number of questions you answer correctly. You should try to answer all the questions, even if you are not sure on the correct answer.

The BCAT has a time limit. The time limit is 55 minutes, of which there are 60 questions in total. You need to make sure that you work quickly and efficiently through the questions, without sacrificing accuracy.

HOW AM I SCORED?

At the end of your BCAT, you will receive your score. Candidates will receive a computer generated feedback sheet on the day of their test. On the feedback sheet, candidates will either receive a 'pass', a 'marginal fail' or a 'significant fail'.

A 'pass' mark means that you are now able to enrol onto the Bar Professional Training Course (BPTC). However, people who score a 'significant fail' may want to reconsider their next step. This test is a mere indication of the level of difficulty to expect from the BPTC; however this course will be notably more difficult than the BCAT. If you fail, you may need to reconsider whether the job of a barrister is ideal for you.

NOTE: we cannot give you an exact number of how many marks you will need in order to pass the BCAT. The number of exact marks is not available, but is claimed by the Bar Standards Board that the grade boundary is set quite low; and the majority of candidates do pass. The pass mark is set quite low in order to filter strong candidates from the weak, and therefore only allowing the candidates who show potential to move on to the next stage of application.

TOP TIPS FOR THE BCAT

In order for you to feel fully prepared for the BCAT, you need to be able to demonstrate high levels of critical thinking and other core skills. To help you pass your test, we have provided you with a list of tips that may help you focus on everything you will need to know in order to pass the Bar Course Aptitude Test:

- **You need to ask yourself basic questions.** Consider the following: 'what is the situation?', 'what do I know from this?', 'what doesn't this tell me?' and 'what is being taken for granted?' Such questions will allow you to probe deeper into the information and spot errors or assumptions in the information provided.

- **Rate the quality of information.** You need to be able to demonstrate your ability to identify underlying assumptions and the impact this causes on the validity of the information. Rate each assumption by asking questions such as 'how likely is this assumption to be true?', 'how can we assume this to be true?', 'are there any other possible assumptions to take into consideration?'

- **Question your assumptions.** Do they make sense? Look at things from all angles. Don't just rely on your initial assumption. Try and look at other alternatives.

- **Read carefully.** A common mistake amongst these tests is that candidates do not read the question or statement properly. Be sure to take your time on reading everything carefully to ensure you answer the question correctly.

- The "**RED Model**". The "**Red Model**" refers to recognising, evaluating and concluding. Make sure you follow each step. This model will allow you to conduct clear and concise reasoning and demonstrate your critical approach.

- **An objective and balanced approach.** Be sure to look for clear, precise and relevant information. You need to be able to distinguish between what is fact and what is assumed. You need to find evidence to support your claim. You need to be able to remain objective. Take a step back and look at a situation from a retrospective point of view.

- **Evaluate.** Try to identify multiple possibilities based on the evidence and facts you are presented with. Make sure you explore all the important information you are provided with and evaluate its strength in terms of argument validity and accuracy.

Now have a go at the following sample questions to get some idea of what to expect in the BCAT.

SAMPLE QUESTIONS – INFERENCES

The term inference can be used to describe conclusions that can be drawn from supposed facts and observations. Although inferences are based on possible facts, it does by no means provide a correct nor accurate account of the truth; it is a mere depiction of a 'possibility' that may or may not be the truth.

Inferences are an intellectual act by which one can conclude something is true on the basis of something else being true, or seeming to be true. Inferences can be accurate or inaccurate, logical or illogical, justified or unjustified. You simply need to take these inferences at face value and accept what the statement is telling you.

For example, if you pass a house which has its lights on, you could infer that someone is home. However this may not be true. Although the lights may be on, the house may be completely empty. The occupants of the house may have forgotten to turn the lights off. Or maybe they left them on to make it look like someone was home. By all accounts, any of these scenarios could be possibilities and all of these scenarios can therefore be referred to as inferences.

For each inference, you will be given a choice of 5 possible answers: **True, Probably True, Insufficient Data, Probably False and False.**

ANSWER OPTIONS

Tick **True** if you believe the inference follows reasonable logic to the statement provided.

Tick **Probably True if** you think it is more than likely to be true than false, but holds no solid evidence.

Tick **Insufficient Data** if you think that you are unable to tell from the statement provided. You have nothing to base your judgements on.

Tick **Probably False** if you think that it more likely to be false than true.

Tick **False** if you believe that it is wrong because it either misinterprets the facts given or contradicts the statement in some way.

Question 1

Statement:

Woman's organisations in India have welcomed the amendment of the Industrial Employment Rules 1946 to control sexual harassments in the work place.

Proposed Inference:

Sexual harassment in India has become more problematic compared to other developed countries.

True	Probably True	Insufficient Data	Probably False	False

Question 2

Statement:

Woman's organisations in India have welcomed the amendment of the Industrial Employment Rules 1946 to control sexual harassments in the work place.

Proposed Inference:

Women in India have been subject to sexual harassment.

True	Probably True	Insufficient Data	Probably False	False

Question 3

Statement:

It would be in everyone's interest to make CVs anonymous in order to give everyone the same equal chance. It is argued that name, gender, photographs, race etc, should all be removed so candidates are selected based on performance, skill and experience.

Proposed Inference:

The argument is based on minimising discrimination based on gender, race and appearance.

True	Probably True	Insufficient Data	Probably False	False

Question 4

Statement:

The case of a Mumbai couple who approached the courts in India after their time limit for an abortion was overdue, wanted a termination of their pregnancy. This case of euthanasia was denied by the courts. The parents wanted to be granted permission for an abortion after they found out that the foetus had been detected to have disabilities which would affect the life of the unborn child. The courts argued that the unborn child had the right to live despite being possibly disabled.

Proposed Inference:

The courts in India have the right and authority to sanction euthanasia.

True	Probably True	Insufficient Data	Probably False	False

Question 5

Statement:

The case of a Mumbai couple who approached the courts in India after their time limit for an abortion was overdue, wanted a termination of their pregnancy. This case of euthanasia was denied by the courts. The parents wanted to be granted permission for an abortion after they found out that the foetus had been detected to have disabilities which would affect the life of the unborn child. The courts argued that the unborn child had the right to live despite being possibly disabled.

Proposed Inference:

The courts consider how far along a woman is in her pregnancy before granting permission for terminating a pregnancy.

True	Probably True	Insufficient Data	Probably False	False

Question 6

Statement:

The case of a Mumbai couple who approached the courts in India after their time limit for an abortion was overdue, wanted a termination of their pregnancy. This case of euthanasia was denied by the courts. The parents wanted to be granted permission for an abortion after they found out that the foetus had been detected to have disabilities which would affect the life of the unborn child. The courts argued that the unborn child has the right to live despite being possibly disabled.

Proposed Inference:

The courts of Mumbai believe that the child had no rights because it was unborn.

True	Probably True	Insufficient Data	Probably False	False

SAMPLE QUESTIONS - RECOGNITION OF ASSUMPTIONS

Assumptions rely on the idea that something is presupposed and therefore, taken for granted.

Assumptions are not always correct, or justifiable. They are something that we take at face value. They form part of our belief system. We assume our beliefs to be true and use them to interpret other things accordingly.

You need to be able to distinguish the difference between inferences and assumptions. As discussed earlier, inferences are a way to conclude whether a statement is true based on something else being true. Whereas, assumptions are something that we learn from prior experience or knowledge and therefore believe it to be true, despite it not necessarily being the case.

For each proposed assumption, you will be given a choice of 2 possible answers: **Assumption Made** and **Assumption Not Made**.

ANSWER OPTIONS

Tick **Assumption Made** if you believe that the assumption can be made from the statement provided.
Tick **Assumption Not Made** if you think that the assumption does not follow and is not necessarily an assumption that can be made or assumed from the statement provided.

Question 1

Statement:

We want to get to our holiday destination in the quickest possible time, so we will go by plane.

Proposed Assumption:

There is a flight service available to get to their destination.

Assumption Made	Assumption Not Made

Question 2

Statement:

We want to get to our holiday destination in the quickest possible time, so we will go by plane.

Proposed Assumption:

Going by plane is the fastest way to travel.

Assumption Made	Assumption Not Made

Question 3

Statement:

The aim of education is to create an efficient and capable workforce.

Proposed Assumption:

Education is the only way which ensures society of compliant workers.

Assumption Made	Assumption Not Made

Question 4

Statement:

The students from Chile demanded that university education should be free. In 2012, they formed a protest around this topic.

Proposed Assumption:

Students from Chile are unable to afford to go to university to receive a higher education.

Assumption Made	Assumption Not Made

Question 5

Statement:

The students from Chile demanded that university education should be free. In 2012, they formed a protest around this topic.

Proposed Assumption:

Other universities outside Chile are free.

Assumption Made	Assumption Not Made

Question 6

Statement:

The students from Chile demanded that university education should be free. In 2012, they formed a protest around this topic.

Proposed Assumption:

The Chilean students had strong views about the cost of university.

Assumption Made	Assumption Not Made

SAMPLE QUESTIONS – DEDUCTION

Deduction is a way of eliminating the wrong answers from the right one. The aim of this test is to demonstrate your level of critical thinking and how you interpret the information you are provided with.

For this test, you need to carefully read through each statement and conclusion and work out whether the conclusion can be made from the previous statement. For these statements, you need to take them at face value. Consider each statement as true, regardless of what you believe. You need to try and not let your personal judgement interfere with your answers. You need to answer based only on the information you are provided with and not what you know to be true.

For each statement, you will be given a choice of 2 possible answers: **Conclusion Follows** and **Conclusion Does Not Follow.**

ANSWER OPTIONS

Tick **Conclusion Follows** if you believe the conclusion does follow on from the statement and therefore provides a logical outcome. Tick **Conclusion Does Not Follow** if you think that the conclusion does not necessarily follow on from the statement and therefore provides an illogical overview of the facts provided.

Question 1

Statement:

Workers are either practical or theoretical. If people are practical, they are not theoretical.

Proposed Conclusion:

It is impossible for a person to be theoretical if they are already practical.

Conclusion Follows	Conclusion Does Not Follow

Question 2

Statement:

Workers are either practical or theoretical. If people are practical, they are not theoretical.

Proposed Conclusion:

Jack works in design, therefore he must be practical.

Conclusion Follows	Conclusion Does Not Follow

Question 3

Statement:

Companies are expanding their presence on the web. Most companies believe that in order to succeed they should devote more time in web designing and SEO. However, it is obvious that companies are more likely to succeed if they pay attention to data management and social networking.

Proposed Conclusion:
Only companies that devote their time in social networking and data management will succeed.

Conclusion Follows	Conclusion Does Not Follow

Question 4

Statement:
Companies are expanding their presence on the web. Most companies believe that in order to succeed they should devote more time in web designing and SEO. However, it is obvious that companies are more likely to succeed if they pay attention to data management and social networking.

Proposed Conclusion:
No company is spending time on web design and SEO.

Conclusion Follows	Conclusion Does Not Follow

Question 5

Statement:

Companies are expanding their presence on the web. Most companies believe that in order to succeed they should devote more time in web designing and SEO. However, it is obvious that companies are more likely to succeed if they pay attention to data management and social networking.

Proposed Conclusion:

Data management is more important than web design.

Conclusion Follows	Conclusion Does Not Follow

Question 6

Statement:

People in poverty suffer multiple physical illnesses. All people with multiple physical illnesses are unhappy.

Proposed Conclusion:

People who are happy are not poor.

Conclusion Follows	Conclusion Does Not Follow

SAMPLE QUESTIONS – INTERPRETATION

Interpretation is a way of explaining the meaning of something. You need to be able to show that you can critically engage with a passage or information, and interpret the information to form a solid conclusion.

For this test, you need to carefully read through each statement and then read each proposed conclusion. You will need to determine whether the proposed conclusion you are given follows on from the statement provided. In other words, can the conclusion be reached from what you have just read?

For these statements, you are to regard them as true. You need to try and not let your own prejudice interfere with your answers in order to provide accurate results.

For each statement, you will be given a choice of 2 possible answers: **Conclusion Follows** and **Conclusion Does Not Follow.**

ANSWER OPTIONS

Tick **Conclusion Follows** if you believe the conclusion does follow on from the statement and therefore provides a logical outcome. Tick **Conclusion Does Not Follow** if you think that the conclusion does not necessarily follow on from the statement and therefore provides an illogical overview of the facts provided.

Question 1

Statement:

A company was looking for ways to cut expenses. In an attempt to do so, the business let go of their advertising department and outsourced their advertising needs from an advertising company. This would allow the company to save 25% for the year on its advertising expenses.

Proposed Conclusion:

The company has been able to save ¼ of their advertising expenditures by outsourcing their advertising requirements.

Conclusion Follows	Conclusion Does Not Follow

Question 2

Statement:

A company was looking for ways to cut expenses. In an attempt to do so, the business let go of their advertising department and outsourced their advertising needs from an advertising company. This would allow the company to save 25% for the year on its advertising expenses.

Proposed Conclusion:

The company saved 25% by outsourcing one of their departments. If other companies were to do the same, they too would save money.

Conclusion Follows	Conclusion Does Not Follow

Question 3

Statement:

A new fashion company is opening. It is often said that new companies are more likely to fail in the first two years of opening as opposed to well-established companies that have been around for several years.

Proposed Conclusion:

Well-established companies will not fail or close down.

Conclusion Follows	Conclusion Does Not Follow

Question 4

Statement:

A new fashion company is opening. It is often said that new companies are more likely to fail in the first two years of opening as opposed to well-established companies that have been around for several years.

Proposed Conclusion:

Well-established companies stand a bigger chance of succeeding as opposed to newer companies that struggle in their first two years of opening.

Conclusion Follows	Conclusion Does Not Follow

Question 5

Statement:

The South East and Central Southern England had a record rainfall of 175.2 mm in January 2014 – beating the previous record of 158.2 mm in 1988. Generally, predictions of rainfall and weather conditions are often inaccurate and prove extremely difficult to predict the outcome.

Proposed Conclusion:

The rainfall in 2014 was not predicted by weather forecasters.

Conclusion Follows	Conclusion Does Not Follow

Question 6

Statement:

The South East and Central Southern England had a record rainfall of 175.2 mm in January 2014 – beating the previous record of 158.2 mm in 1988. Predictions of rainfall and weather conditions are often inaccurate and prove extremely difficult to predict the outcome.

Proposed Conclusion:

The rainfall in 1988 for South East and Central Sothern England was less than that of 2014.

Conclusion Follows	Conclusion Does Not Follow

SAMPLE QUESTIONS – EVALUATION OF ARGUMENTS

The last type of question in your BCAT is **evaluation of arguments.** The role of a barrister is to make important decisions and distinguish between strong and weak arguments, data and evidence. This is exactly what this test will entail.

For each question, you will be presented with either a statement or question which you are to regard as fact. You will then be given a proposed argument. This proposed argument will either agree or disagree with what has been said. The difficulty comes next, in which you must read each proposed argument carefully and identify whether it is a strong or weak argument.

For each statement, you will be given a choice of 2 possible answers: **Argument Strong** and **Argument Weak**.

ANSWER OPTIONS

Tick **Argument Strong** if you believe the argument is both significant and direct in relation to the question.
Tick **Argument Weak** if you think that the argument is not strong enough to work. If it does not directly relate to the question, or only shows minor importance or relativity to the argument, you are to regard the argument as weak.

Question 1

Statement:

Should parents encourage their children to participate in extra activities and learning programmes, in order to reach their full learning potential?

Proposed Argument:

Yes; parents have the responsibility to help their children succeed in whatever they want to do in life.

Argument Strong	Argument Weak

Question 2

Statement:

Should parents encourage their children to participate in extra activities and learning programmes, in order to reach their full learning potential?

Proposed Argument:

Yes; extra activities and learning programmes are a great way for children to reach their full learning ability. They will provide useful skills, knowledge and talents that will help them develop in their learning process.

Argument Strong	Argument Weak

Question 3

Statement:

Should parents encourage their children to participate in extra activities and learning programmes, in order to reach their full learning potential?

Proposed Argument:

No; children who want to learn will do so. Children do not want to feel pressurised in doing something they might end up resenting their parents for. Children will develop in their own time and in their own way.

Argument Strong	Argument Weak

Question 4

Statement:

Should the Government allow convicted criminals the right to expunge their criminal record after 5 years of good behaviour after being released?

Proposed Argument:

No; the Government will be criticised for their lack of authority.

Argument Strong	Argument Weak

Question 5

Statement:

Should the Government allow convicted criminals the right to expunge their criminal record after 5 years of being sentenced?

Proposed Argument:

Yes; everyone has the right for a second chance.

Argument Strong	Argument Weak

Question 6

Statement:

Should the Government allow convicted criminals the right to expunge their criminal record after 5 years of being sentenced?

Proposed Argument:

Yes, allowing expulsion of criminal records will allow convicted criminals the opportunity to become rehabilitated and adjust better in society.

Argument Strong	Argument Weak

ANSWERS TO BCAT

INFERENCES

Q1.

Insufficient data: there is no evidence to suggest whether this is true or false. You cannot tell from the facts given. One can assume that there are more sexual harassment problems in India compared to other developed countries, but we have no data to suggest how much harassment goes on India, and how this differs from other developed countries.

Q2.

Probably True. If a sexual harassment law has been welcomed into the country, this suggests that there was a need to bring it in, and that women were being subject to sexual harassment.

Q3.

True. The aim of this argument is to reduce the risk of discrimination based on race, gender and appearance. This claim is beyond reasonable to make based on the data provided.

Q4.

True. The couple went to the courts because they have the power to sanction euthanasia and therefore the inference must be true.

Q5.

Probably true. The courts are more than likely to take into consideration how far along the woman is in her pregnancy before granting permission for an abortion. However, there is no solid evidence to suggest this, so the claim is most probably true.

Q6.

False. The statement clearly indicates that the courts believe "that the unborn child has rights to live despite being possibly disabled". So therefore, this proposed claim is false.

RECOGNITION OF ASSUMPTIONS

Q1.

Assumption made. For them to go by plane it must be possible to get a flight, so therefore this is necessarily assumed from the statement provided.

Q2.

Assumption made. It is assumed by the statement provided that going by plane is the quickest means of transportation compared to other transportation services, so therefore the assumption can be made.

Q3.

Assumption not made. It cannot be assumed that the only way to create compliant workers is through education.

Q4.

Assumption not made. The statement does not talk about students being unable to pay for university. The assumption is not referred to in the statement and therefore cannot be made.

Q5.

Assumption not made. The statement does not refer to other universities. The assumption to change university fees to being free of charge cannot be assumed.

Q6.

Assumption made. The statement refers to a student protest regarding university prices. This therefore assumes that the students had something to say and felt strongly about the issue.

DEDUCTION

Q1.

Conclusion follows. It is stated in the sentence that if people are practical, they are not going to be theoretical. Therefore the conclusion follows in that a person cannot be theoretical if they are already practical.

Q2.

Conclusion does not follow. This generalises the statement. We cannot know from Jack's occupation of working in design whether or not he is practical or theoretical, we could assume it would most likely be practical and 'hands on', but that is a significant assumption to make.

Q3.

Conclusion does not follow. The use of the word 'only' makes the conclusion false. The use of the words 'far more likely' means a possibility, it is not set in stone, and therefore the conclusion cannot follow.

Q4.

Conclusion does not follow. Again, this conclusion cannot follow the statement. The statement does not mention anything in regards to what other companies are spending their time on.

Q5.

Conclusion does not follow. You cannot tell whether data management is more important than web design. The statement uses data management and social networking and web design and SEO to make the comparison. You cannot tell whether one makes the other one more important, when it compares four elements.

Q6.

Conclusion does not follow. Just because people with multiple physical illnesses are unhappy, does not mean that people who are happy are not poor.

INTERPRETATION

Q1.

Conclusion follows. The company has saved 25% on their advertising requirements by outsourcing the advertising department to a local advertising company. So, their 25% (1/4) of the business's expenditures have been saved, so therefore the conclusion follows from the statement provided.

Q2.

Conclusion does not follow. The statement does not indicate that other businesses could prosper by outsourcing one of their departments. The statement only talks about the company's profits, it is by no means of a way to indicate the prosperities of other companies, so therefore the conclusion does not follow.

Q3.

Conclusion does not follow. The statement talks about the difference between new companies and well-established companies. It does not indicate any possibility that well-established companies cannot or will not fail. This cannot be assumed from the statement provided, so therefore the conclusion does not follow.

Q4.

Conclusion follows. The statement suggests that new companies are more likely to fail as opposed to well-established companies. The conclusion follows in that it demonstrates how well-established companies have a better chance of succeeding and surviving in comparison to newer companies.

Q5.

Conclusion does not follow. The statement shows no indication of whether or not the forecasters were able to predict the rainfall of 2014 correctly. Therefore, the conclusion cannot be drawn from the statement provided.

Q6.

Conclusion follows. The statement suggests that the rainfall in January 2014 was greater than the rainfall in 1988, which clearly illustrates that the conclusion follows on from the statement provided.

EVALUATION OF ARGUMENTS

Q1.

Argument weak. This argument lacks the direct link back to the statement in question. The statement identifies extra activities and learning programmes as possible ways in which their children can reach their full learning potential. However, the argument does not mention these possible ways to achieve success, and 'help them to achieve whatever' seems a little vague in terms of children reaching their maximum learning potential.

Q2.

Argument strong. The argument links directly back to the statement. It talks about the examples of extra activities and learning programmes as a way of increasing a child's learning abilities. The argument also gives ways in which it can help reach their potential through learning new skills and talents, which provides a solid argument for parents to encourage their children.

Q3.

Argument strong. The argument targets both the action being presented and the consequences of their actions. It states that parents shouldn't encourage their children to participate in such programmes and activities and gives reasons as to why. This links back to the initial action of getting parents to encourage their children and giving clear and concise examples as to why they shouldn't.

Q4.

Argument weak. This argument is weak because it does not clarify any specific reasons to back up the opinion that they shouldn't expunge their criminal records. Just because they might be criticised, this does not deal with the overall statement.

Q5.

Argument weak. This argument does not offer any insight into the initial statement provided. There is no clear link between the statement and the argument. The argument only works on beliefs and emotions. There is no solid ground to work with in terms of a valid argument. The argument mentions second chances; it does not refer to the expunging of criminal records and therefore there is missing information in this argument which makes it weak.

Q6.

Argument strong. The argument shows a clear link between the statement provided and the proposed argument. The argument mentions the supposed action (expunging of criminal records) and the possible consequences that could take place in relation to the action. It relates the action to a positive effect which it could have, therefore producing an important and strong argument.

For more practice questions for the BCAT, please visit www.how2become.com or go on to Amazon and search 'How2become Bar Course Aptitude Tests'.

CHAPTER 8

IMPROVING YOUR CHANCES

In between school and university or after completion of the academic stage of training, it is important to try and obtain some relevant work experience. As the profession is very competitive even a short stint in a work based environment may give you an edge over your competitors. The most important work experience a budding barrister can obtain is called a 'mini-pupillage'.

MINI-PUPILLAGE

This takes place at a barristers' Chambers, a place where barristers sit together and work, and any individual can make an application for one. You need to apply directly to the Chambers and the application should be strong if you wish to be considered.

The length of the mini-pupillage could vary depending on the set of Chambers but usually lasts a week in total. This time could be spent shadowing a barrister and learning how he or she spends her time. If allowed, there may be visits to court too and the chance to sit with a barrister during a court case they are involved in.

You are allowed to do more than one mini-pupillage and most Chambers would want to see at least one for the purpose of the pupillage application. You should check the website of individual Chambers to see what their requirements for making such an application are.

The other benefits of this experience are as follows;

- You may be able to focus on a particular area of law you are interested in practising in the future;
- You can see the day-to-day workings of a practising barrister;
- It will give you an advantage over other applicants at the academic and vocational stage;
- There may be some individuals that you make contact with for future applications, references and assistance with securing pupillages;
- You could decide at a relatively early stage that this profession is not for you without spending thousands of pounds and valuable time on courses.

Some Chambers may require you to complete an assessed mini-pupillage before being accepted on a full pupillage. You can check the 'Pupil Gateway' website for mini-pupillage vacancies.

A mini-pupillage is a pre-requisite for all students wishing to train as a barrister. The application to Chambers must be very strong as competition for positions is fierce.

There are other forms of useful work experience which may also assist in obtaining a pupillage. You should make note of these when considering your work experience prior to your pupillage.

MARSHALLING

Marshalling is where you sit with a judge at court for a period of time and get to watch a case in action.

SOLICITOR'S FIRM

Work experience, either paid or unpaid, at a solicitor's firm may be the key to getting an insight into the profession. A lot of the legal work may be similar but seeing the front line work involving contact with clients is very useful.

PARALEGEL WORK AND OUTDOOR CLERKING

Paralegal work could be at a local firm of a solicitors and usually involves assisting with case preparation and also legal research or other administrative duties. You can apply for paralegal work using your CV. They may also ask for a Covering Letter to go alongside your CV, so you need to make sure these are strong (*see Creating your CV for more information*).

> **Remember, pro bono work will not only allow you to help those who cannot afford to pay the fees of a solicitor, but it helps you to gain much needed knowledge and skills that will allow you to be a better, more experienced solicitor.**

VOLUNTARY WORK

This may be at your local citizens' advice bureau where you advise clients for free without any sort of remuneration for your time. Alternatively, it may involve working at a local law centre or not-for-profit organisation. It is also referred to as 'pro bono' work and is looked upon favourably on your CV. This will undoubtedly improve your chances of being successful.

Pro bono work

Pro bono work is essentially a way of helping people who are unable to afford legal fees and work for free. Think of it as work experience. The added benefit of pro bono is that it will help a barrister to develop the core skills of client care and case management. Another reason pro bono work is a good thing is that there are people out there who need the help but just can't afford it. While you are building your skills doing this type of work, you are helping others in need and allowing others to see the good side of those in the legal profession.

Remember, pro bono work will not only allow you to help those who cannot afford to pay the fees of a barrister, but it helps you to gain much needed knowledge and skills that will allow you to be a better, more experienced solicitor.

Pro bono work is becoming more and more popular among young lawyers. Many aspiring barristers are now seeing the benefit of performing pro bono work.

For more information regarding pro bono work, please visit the following website: www.barprobono.org.uk.

GIVING YOURSELF THE BEST CHANCE

1. Ensure that you have a strong CV when applying for your pupillage. Your CV should contain ALL of your relevant academic achievements and work experience.

2. Choose relevant subjects for your A-levels to ensure that you get into the university of your choice. If you have already done you're a-levels, you need to come up with reasons as to how you can apply the skills you achieved from that subject to a law degree.

3. Aim for a top classification at university. Either a first class or upper second class degree is desired in order to get into a good BPTC course.

4. Prepare thoroughly for your pupillage interview by reviewing your application before the interview.

5. Decide on which particular area of law you are interested in before applying to Chambers.

6. Make sure you have arranged funding for your legal training. Remember, training to be a lawyer is expensive. There are loads of options to help you finance your education.

7. Practice and prepare for the BCAT and join an Inn of Court in order to apply for a place on the BPTC course.

8. Get as much work experience as possible before you complete the academic part of your training.

9. Develop a wide range of interests to make yourself more well-rounded and attractive during your pupillage interview.

10. Compete in mooting and debating events at university and school.

KEY POINTS

- Work experience can be obtained during or after school, at university or at the end of the academic stage.
- All relevant work experience can be useful for the vocational stage of training and to help you qualify as a barrister.
- Working at a solicitors' firm may be a useful place to start and is relevant even for trainee barristers.
- Marshalling and visits to court are beneficial in getting a better insight in how it works and the process involved.
- Mini-pupillages take place at Chambers and are a pre-requisite to obtaining a pupillage.

CHAPTER 9

CREATING YOUR CV

After gaining the correct educational qualifications and completing the required vocational training, you will be able to start applying for job positions as a barrister.

Finding the right job can be extremely difficult, and with the job market being more competitive than ever before, you need to maximise your chances and give yourself a head start.

This head start all begins with perfecting your CV.

WHAT IS A CV?

CV stands for 'Curriculum Vitae', and is another name for a resume. Your CV will tell a future employer everything they need to know about you in order to make an informed decision as to whether or not you are the right person for the position.

CVs are the most important marketing tool you will use to help sell yourself, so you need to understand the importance of conducting a great CV.

Before creating your CV, you should first research the Chambers or organisation you are applying for a job with. This will help you to know which of your skills you will want to highlight according to what they are looking for.

WHAT YOU SHOULD DO:

- Make sure that it is easy to read, clearly laid out in a logical order, and that you haven't tried to cram in too much. Usually 2 pages is sufficient enough.
- Make sure that it is informative and that it isn't cluttered with information not relevant to the position you are applying for.
- Make sure you account for any gaps in your employment history. For example, if you were travelling or took time off to further your education, you should list those instances and explain what you gained from those experiences.
- Make sure that you include your entire schooling history including dates and grades. If you leave your grades off, the employer will be left to assume that they are sub-par.
- Make sure that you include your qualification date, either confirmed or pending, and the jurisdiction. (Also include whether you require or hold a visa to work in the UK).
- Make sure that you include any extra training courses you have taken and any articles you have written or contributed to, as well as any seminars, debates or marketing activities you have been involved in.
- Make sure that it is free of grammatical and spelling errors.

Generally you will have between THREE and SIX seconds to grab the employer's attention, in hope for them to continue reading and entice them with your skills, knowledge and personality.

WHAT YOU SHOULD AVOID:

- Don't use the words CV or Resume on your document. The employer knows what it is, and it takes up valuable space that could be used to show your talent.
- Don't make your CV more than two pages long. Generally speaking, a potential employer will be busy and will not have time to read a lengthy history.
- Don't include work experience that is not relevant to the position you are applying for.
- Don't exaggerate your educational or work experience. If you do so, you will likely be found out at some point.
- Don't include personal information such as religion, marital status, ethnicity or age.
- Don't have your CV printed on both sides of a page. Each page is important and should be on its own sheet of paper.
- Don't fold your CV. A clean, creaseless CV is more appealing to the eye. Keep your CV in a folder so that you can hand it to a potential employer. If you are mailing a CV, mail it in an envelope large enough that you will not need to fold it.

THE LAYOUT OF YOUR CV

You may think that the format of your CV is not that important to a potential employer; think again! Employers can tell a great deal about a person based on the 'look' and the 'feel' of a CV. That is why you must make sure you convey yourself professionally, intellectually and stylistically.

Your CV needs to be pleasing on the eye. Before the employer even knows who you are, they will scan over your CV and form a quick opinion about you. That opinion needs to be positive. The way you present yourself on paper will determine whether or not the employer wants to invite you to an interview.

REMEMBER: A good CV is crucial for securing a pupillage and even a job. Alongside the completed application, it gives the Chambers an opportunity to see what the applicant has to offer and what his or her qualifications and experience are.

Below I have provided you with an example of a strong CV for the pupillage application. Use this to generate some ideas for your own CV. Remember, your CV needs to be tailored to your key strengths, qualities and skills.

(NAME)

(Address)

Mobile: E-mail:

PERSONAL STATEMENT

I am a highly motivated and driven individual with a lot of ambition. I have achieved a good classification in my law degree and will pursue my goal to become a commercial barrister in London. I spent some weeks completing two mini-pupillages at a London Chambers to help gain experience and decide on an area of law that I was interested in. I have successfully competed in mooting competitions at university and am secretary for the law society.

EDUCATION

2000- 2013 Liverpool University

LL.B Law with honours 2:1

First Year: *Contract Law (Pass), Land Law (Merit), Constitutional and Administrative Law (Merit)*

Second Year: *Property (69%), Obligations (75%)*

Final Year: *Media, Employment, Clinical Negligence, Human Rights*

1993-2000 Holy Trinity School, London

3 A levels: *History (B), Politics (A) and English (B)*

9 A-C's GCSE's: *including A*s in Art and English literature, 5B's and 2C's.*

LEGAL EXPERIENCE

Free Representation Unit- London 2014

I have spent 12 months working at a free representation unit in London. I gained valuable experience in housing law and drafted many legal documents. I worked under the guidance of a very senior solicitor.

Marshalling- August 2013

I was fortunate enough to spend four days marshalling in London Crown Court and London Magistrates Court.

Mini pupillages

Old Temple Chambers- London May 2014
Sussex Chambers

I also completed two mini-pupillages at a large Chambers, working closely with highly experienced barristers. I attended court with barristers and conducted legal research. I was able to draft some documents after conducting legal research which was used as part of the trial bundle.

Mooting- January 2015

Won the law school mooting competition with my partner at the regional university finals.

Mid Temple

Member as a student and attended dinners which allowed me to network with barristers.

INTERESTS

- President of local public speakers club.
- Member of local hockey club.
- Fund raising events organised for children's charity.

SKILLS

- Microsoft word and excel.
- Clean and full driving licence.
- Use of Westlaw and LexisNexis.
- Able to read and write in Spanish.

REFERENCES

Available on request

As you can see, the CV is formatted in a clear, concise and grammatically correct manner, in order to convey yourself as professional and articulate.

WHY DO PEOPLE FAIL AT THIS STAGE?

The submission of a CV is usually the initial stage of any selection process. Most employers will place a job advert in a newspaper or online with brief details of the job attached inviting people to apply for the post by way of submitting their CV.

The vast majority of these people will send off a 'generic' CV by email, and then wonder why they never receive a reply. As I mentioned earlier, your CV needs to be specific!

Employers are very busy people and as such, you need to make your CV as appealing and as effective as possible. If you do this, they will notice your CV and you will get shortlisted and invited to an interview.

There are a few things that you can in order to make sure that your CV is effective. Most importantly, and I cannot stress this enough, is to MATCH the person specification and requirements of the job in which you've applied for.

Remember, your CV should be used as a tool to assist you during the selection process, and therefore it should be centred on the following areas:

- Creating the right impression of yourself.
- Indicating that you possess the right qualities and attributes to

perform the role of the job you are applying for.

- Grabbing the employer's attention.
- Being concise, succinct and clear.
- Providing evidence, where possible, of relevant skills, qualities, experience and qualifications.

AN EFFECTIVE CV

The most effective CVs are the ones that make the assessors job easy. They are simple to read, straight to the point, relevant, and focus on the job role which has been advertised.

Effective CV writing is an acquired skill that can be obtained relatively quickly with a little bit of time, effort and focus.

I have provided you with some space on the following pages to draft a strong CV that you can use to apply for pupillage as a barrister.

(Consider everything that has been discussed in this chapter, and remember to include ALL of your key strengths and qualities. Your CV should make you sound GREAT! I have provided all of the headings that you should include in your CV

Name:

Address:

Mobile: Email:

PERSONAL PROFILE

EDUCATION

LEGAL EXPERIENCE

INTERESTS

SKILLS

REFERENCES

CHAPTER 10

THE APPLICATION FORM

The application form is one of the most crucial stages to the application process of becoming a barrister. The level of research and the effort which needs to be put into your application form is imperative.

When submitting application forms, it is important to produce a quality, professional and detailed application form to make you shine. It is the first time that you will get to make an impression and try to stand out from all of the other applicants.

The main aim of the application form is to show all the necessary information which they employers want to see. Take note that application forms are often long winded and can be quite daunting.

The forms ask for a great deal of detail and research, so it is absolutely essential that your response is highly driven, full of detailed support and information, and clearly illustrates all your best abilities to enhance your application over others.

Amongst your application form, you may be required to submit your CV and a Covering Letter. I have already gone through the CV in the previous chapter, so make sure you read through this section carefully.

COVERING LETTER

A Covering Letter is a written document that you can attach to your CV to provide further insight into why you are applying for the job position. This can be given a word limit, so you need to find out what the word limit is in order to construct a strong covering letter.

When applying to a job by mail or even through a website, you will need to include a covering letter. Your Covering Letter is your absolute first impression on any employer, and will explain your reasons for becoming a barrister and why you are applying for the position.

In order for your Cover Letter to be effective in making the reader want to continue on to looking at your CV, you must have a clear structure. It is not uncommon for employers to read a Cover Letter and not even go on to look at the CV or job application. You must impress them first with your cover letter and make them want to know more about you.

<u>If you are applying pupillage, your Covering Letter should include the following:</u>

- **The opening.** This is an introduction and here you should explain who you are and why you are applying for the job position. This portion of your Cover Letter should only be one or two sentences.

- **Why?** Your second paragraph should explain why you want to be a barrister and why you want this job. Here you would also explain any experiences you've had that brought you to the decision to be a barrister. This may include pro bono work, work experience and even mini-pupillages. By providing this information will impress recruiters when they see the effort you put forth into comparing the two sides of the legal profession. You also want to make it clear why you want to work in the area of law that the firm focuses on. This is a great chance to show off any research you have done by explaining your interest in their main practice areas. Be sure to provide evidence of your interest.

- **Why you?** This is the section where you get to pitch yourself to the recruiter. You will want to make it clear that you are suited to a career as a barrister Highlight any achievements that show you have the competence they are looking for. If your covering letter is attached to an actual job application, be careful to only repeat information you filled out on the application that is most significant. Be as broad as possible.

- **The ending.** Here you want to close your letter, referring the recruiter to your CV and stating your availability for an interview.

FORMAT OF A COVERING LETTER

Overall, your covering letter should be no longer than one page. Keep it professional, using a font size of 11 or 12. Never rush to send it to the recruiter. Make sure you go over the letter with a fine toothed comb, ensuring that there are no spelling or grammatical errors. If you have the opportunity for someone you know to go over the letter, take that route. This will ensure that the cover letter is professional, clean and accurate.

The point of a covering letter is to highlight the reasoning why you are applying for the job position. Information that you should focus on within a covering letter is:

- Why you have chosen to become a barrister;
- Why you have applied for the job;
- Why you make a good candidate. (Skills, experience, qualities);
- Other interests and skills that enhance your application.

Remember, you must tailor your answers to each application you fill out in a different way. Each job has its own unique style and so, what fits for one recruiter, maybe slightly different to another.

THE USE OF KEYWORDS

Using positive keywords and phrases when completing your application form betters your chances of success. As human beings, we naturally respond in a position manner to certain words and phrases and we also react negatively to others.

<u>Below is a list of keywords that you may choose to use when completing the responses to your application form.</u>

Enthusiastic
"I am a driven, hardworking and enthusiastic team player"

Dedicated
"I am totally committed to my work and have a track record for being

dedicated, professional, and conscientious."

Punctual
"I fully understand how important it is to be punctual for all work commitments and meetings."

Conscientious
"My peers would describe me as someone who is highly conscientious in the workplace and who can be relied upon to deliver."

Teamwork
"Teamwork is the foundation of any successful business and as an employee of your company, I would always do my utmost to work effectively as a team player."

Proactive
"I am a highly proactive person who is always looking for ways to improve both myself and the company that I am working for."

Focused
"I am a naturally focused person who always decides at the beginning of the day exactly what it is I aim to achieve by the end of the working day. I then go all out to achieve it."

Meticulous
"I am a meticulous person who likes to check over my work once complete to verify its professionalism."

Organised

"I always ensure that I am organised and plan for the next working day's activities."

Persist

"If ever I am unsure how to carry out a task, I will persist until I am fully competent in that particular area."

Adaptable

"Although I am skilled in one particular area, I am extremely adaptable and can be relied upon to assist or change roles at a moment's notice."

Balanced

"My balanced view on things allows me to remain calm in a crisis and always perform to the best of my ability."

Knowledgeable

"I always ensure that I keep myself up-to-date with work related knowledge and information that allows me to perform to the best of my abilities."

Consistent

"I am consistent in all work related activities which ensures that the work I produce is to an exceptional standard."

Analytical

"Having an analytical nature means that I am capable of helping the team solve any problems that may arise."

Independent

Although I am an excellent team worker, I am also sufficiently independent and can be relied upon to work unsupervised when required."

Co-operative

"I fully appreciate how important teamwork is in any given work related situation and I can be relied upon to be co-operative and professional at all times."

The above list is certainly not exhaustive, however, when completing an application form, it is important to reflect yourself in a positive light. This way, possible employers are more likely to accept your application based on a highly positive and professional application that allows you to reflect your own skills, qualities and attributes.

In addition to a CV, the application should also include a good quality Covering Letter to the chosen chambers.

On the following page is a sample Cover Letter to a Chambers for pupillage.

SAMPLE COVERING LETTER

(Your name)
(Your address)

(Employers name)

(Employers address)

Date

Dear Mr Jones,

I am a BVC student at the London Institute for Legal Studies writing to apply for a pupillage at 2 Law Chambers for 20015-16. I graduated from Birmingham University (LLB) in 20014 and thereafter spent some time working in a local Legal advice centre. I enclose my CV with this covering letter.

I am applying to 2 Law Chambers because of your outstanding work in family law. I have read a lot about some of the highly successful barristers working at your chambers and about some of the cases that they have been successful in. I also was able to meet and introduce myself to one of the senior barristers at a dinner for legal students.

I was fortunate enough to complete two mini-pupillages at a chambers in London and this provided me with invaluable experience and knowledge. I met many highly talented barristers during my time there and was lucky enough to shadow and occasion assist them. Whilst there I benefited from the chance to draft many documents for counsel, such as particulars, and the documents were used in court for cases. I hope to specialise in family law and obtained a merit in my family law module at university. Both my academic and extracurricular experiences have given me the requisite skills.

Thank you for taking the time to read my application, and I look forward to hearing from you.

Yours sincerely,

(Name)

THE IMPORTANCE OF THE APPLICATION FORM

A lot of time and thought should go into competing the application form for the pupillage as it forms the core of the interview process at Chambers.

It may need to be looked at by a person with some experience of applications such as a lecturer or careers advisor.

Particular attention should be paid to the questionnaire part of the application as the answers may be used in the interview process.
It may seem obvious but attention should be given to spelling and grammar to avoid the application being discarded.

TIPS FOR FILLING OUT THE APPLICATION FORM

- Prepare yourself by doing research on the firm/organisation and their recruitment criteria.
- Be clear on the selection criteria and try to match your skills, experience and knowledge.
- Read through the entire form and follow the instructions exactly as stated.
- Gauge your answers to fit the space provided.
- Do a rough draft to make sure that you can fit your information into the boxes.
- Online forms will specify a word count; this indicates how much detail is required.
- Don't leave gaps on the application. If you travelled for a period of time instead of holding a job, put that down.

SAMPLE APPLICATION FORM

Here is a sample application form for the Pupillage Gateway that needs to be completed for the pupillage.

1. PERSONAL DETAILS
Title
First Name
Middle Name
Last Name
Preferred Name
Address
Town
Region
Postal / Zip Code
Country
Email Address
Home Telephone
Mobile Telephone
Are there are restrictions on your ability to work in the UK? (Give details)

Do you have any special requirements if you are invited to attend a pupillage interview? (Give details)
Dates when you are UNABLE to attend an interview

2. EDUCATION
School Education (add as many as required)
Institution Type
Institution Name
Institution Location
Institution Dates
Qualification Type
Subject and Grades
Higher Education (add as many as required)

Institution Name	
Qualification Title	
Area of Study	
Grade	
Start Date	
Date Awarded	
CPE / GDL	
Studying / Studied for a Legal Degree?	
CPE / GDL Institution	
Course Type	
Grade	
Mode of Study	
Dates	
BVC / BPTC Institution	
Grade Status	
Grade	
Mode of Study	
Dates	
Date / Proposed Date of Call	

3. EMPLOYMENT HISTORY
Legal Employment and Work Experience (add as many entries as required)
Organisation
Position
Employment Status
Dates
Responsibilities (300 words)
Non-Legal Employment and Work Experience (add as many entries as required)
Organisation
Position
Employment Status
Dates
Responsibilities (300 words)

4. OTHER SKILLS
Language Skills (as many as required)
Language
Fluency
Membership of an Inn of Court
Inn of Court
Inn of Court Membership Status
Membership Number
Date From
Other Professional Qualifications (as many as required)
Qualification
Awarding Body
Grade
Details

5. RESPONSIBILITIES, AWARDS AND INTERESTS
Positions of responsibility, prizes and awards
Please provide details of any positions of responsibility you have held (150 words)
Please provide details of any scholarships, awards or prizes you have achieved (150 words)
Interests and recreational activities
Please provide details of your interests and any non-work related involvement. If relevant to your proposed area of practice, please explain in what way. (150 words)

6. REFERENCES
References (x2)
Academic or Work / Personal (one of each)
Name
Position
Organisation
Address
Email
Relationship

7. EXTENUATING CIRCUMSTANCES
Please provide details of any extenuating circumstances, if relevant to your application. (150 words)

8. PUPILLAGE APPLICATION QUESTIONNAIRE
Why do you wish to become a barrister? (150 words)
What areas of practice are you interested in and why? (200 words)
Give reasons for your choice of Chambers (200 words)
Why do you believe you will make a good barrister? (200 words)
Please identify any experiences / skills gained that you believe may help you in your career. (200 words)

As you can see, the last section of the application form contains a pupillage questionnaire. These questions are used so that you can expand on some of your answers, which will allow the recruiter to gain more of an insight into the type of person you are, and whether you are right for the pupillage.

The five questions in the questionnaire should be answered to the best of your ability. Your answers must include any information that you think will INCREASE your chances of being successful.

<u>Let's recap the five questions from the pupillage questionnaire:</u>

- Why do you wish to become a barrister?
- What areas of practice are you interested in and why?
- Give reasons for your choice of Chambers.
- Why do you believe you will make a good barrister?
- Please identify any experiences / skills gained that you believe may help you in your career.

Why do you wish to become a barrister? (150 words)

What areas of practice are you interested in and why? *(200 words)*

Give reasons for your choice of Chambers. *(200 words)*

Why do you believe you will make a good barrister? *(200 words)*

CHAPTER 11

THE INTERVIEW

Getting an interview has become a challenging and competitive field regarding most job roles. Competition is fierce and therefore you need to be fully prepared and demonstrate that you are at your best.

Nobody enjoys the interview process, in fact the majority of people find the whole experience nerve-wracking. You will need to show great levels of knowledge and experience within the law industry and demonstrate good knowledge of the job role you are applying for.

Interviews are a way for you to be able to express yourself at your best. You can get the job despite someone else being more qualified or experienced. This can be achieved if you prepare for the interview and excel your skills and abilities, as well as take pride in how you convey yourself during the interview.

HOW TO SUCCESSFULLY PASS THE INTERVIEW

It is standard practice to ask certain questions at an interview and therefore well worth preparing answers to these in advance. You should also try to think about other questions the interviewer might ask you based on the position itself and your application. In this article we will provide you with some useful tips on how to pass interviews.

The questions asked at the interview will cover areas such as yourself, the job you have applied for and, possibly, specific technical questions about your chosen subject. Some of the following questions may not be relevant if you are applying for your first job after qualifying from university or leaving school.

You may be asked a question at the interview that completely throws you. If water has been provided, take a sip to give you some thinking time. Stay calm and try to think about why the interviewer has asked the question and what are they looking for in you.

Never underestimate the power of a sense of humour but be careful – not everyone finds the same things funny. If you make the interviewer or interviewers laugh they are likely to remember you. It is possible that your interviewer will become your colleague if you are appointed and this is something they are unlikely to forget!

Your interview is your chance to make the employer take notice of who you are and where you fit into their organisation. Be professional. Dress the part. Speak clearly and with an appropriate volume. Shake their hand firmly and smile. Don't talk to them like they are your friend, or they may not be your future employer. Show them that you are the right person to hire.

<u>The following points are essential if you wish to make a good impression during your interview:</u>

- Extensively research the Chambers/organization for which you are interviewing. Use the internet to search not only their website, but to find other articles or write-ups about them. It is important that you know what their predominant field of law is and any major cases that they may have worked on that has made an impact. It will give you an advantage over other candidates if you show full knowledge and interest about the place you are applying to.

- Dress appropriately. Your first impression is what could make or break you. If you show up in jeans and a t-shirt, the partners may not feel you take the position seriously. Your clothing needs to demonstrate your professional and mature demeanor. For men, a suit shows that you are serious about the job and take pride in your appearance and how you convey yourself to others. For women, a skirted suit or conservative dress with a proper hemline will give the same effect. Be professional in your dress, and show up well groomed. These little details may seem simple, but they are important and they are effective.

- Familiarize yourself with some of the questions you may be asked during the interview process. Some examples of questions you will be asked are: What makes you interested in our firm? Why are you interested in your stated area of practice? What are you hoping for in your career? What are your salary expectations?

Questions about salary expectations are generally the most difficult to answer. On one hand, you don't want to over-sell yourself, ask for too high a salary and get passed over because your demands can't be met. On the other hand, nobody wants to under-sell themselves and ask for too little. Finding a good balance is important.

As you prepare for your interview, whether it be a phone interview or a face-to-face interview, you should ask yourself a few questions:

- What are the areas of law that you are really interested in and why?

- What can you offer the Chambers/organization for which you are interviewing?
- Why do you want a career in law?
- Why did you decide to apply for this particular law Chambers/ organization?

Asking yourself these questions will not only lead you to choose firms to apply for that are more appropriate to your interests, but it will help you feel more comfortable with answering questions that are not as straight forward and specifically about your experience.

THE STAR METHOD

The **STAR** method is one way you can prepare for an interview. It works most effectively when preparing responses to situational type interview questions.

The STAR method basically ensures that your responses to the interview questions follow a concise and logical sequence and also makes sure that you cover every possible area.

Situation – At the commencement of my response, I will explain what the situation was and who else was involved. This will be a relatively comprehensive explanation so that the interview fully understands what it is I am trying to explain.
Task – I will explain what the task was. This will basically be an explanation of what had to be done and by whom.
Action – I will then move on and explain what action I specifically took,

and also what action other people took.

Result – I will finally explain what the result was following my actions. It is important to make sure that the result was positive as a direct result of your actions.

Use this method of response in any form of interview, whether that be a telephone interview, a face-to-face interview or a group interview. You need to demonstrate well-structured and logical responses. Using this method not only shows your thought process for each response, but it allows you to take the time and think carefully about each step in the process of your response.

TIPS WHEN ANSWERING INTERVIEW QUESTIONS

Below I have outlined some TOP TIPS you should consider when answering interview questions:

- Always try to be yourself as adopting a different persona is likely to come across as insincere at the interview.

- Honesty is always the best policy. If you don't know the answer to a question say so rather than making something up. Also, lying about previous achievements or experience is always likely to come back to haunt you if you get the job.

- Try to lead the interviewer towards areas of your experience that you want to talk about. Capture their interest and ensure you pause during your answers to give them a chance to expand on their questions.

- Avoid yes/no answers at all costs and try to support your answers with specific examples from your experience. Try to avoid talking too much otherwise you may be in danger of talking yourself out of a job

- Focus on your strengths and successes wherever possible, but remember the interviewer will want to know that you can also recognise your weaknesses and devise strategies to resolve them through ongoing learning and development of your skills. If you have not had much work experience, you can always use examples from things you do outside of work or university e.g. voluntary work, hobbies etc.

- Many job adverts include details of a salary range for the vacancy in question. However, quite often the question of salary and other employment issues will be discussed towards the end of the interview. One way to raise the subject is to ask how your experience and skills will be recognised in the new role.

- Quite often you will be asked at the end of the interview if you have any questions. If possible hold back one or two that could have been asked during the interview for this purpose. If you have not been told during the interview it is always a good idea to ask when you will be told the outcome of the interview.

- If you do not get the position, you should ask for feedback on how your interview went. This is great way to refine and improve your interview technique.

- Whenever possible, end the interview on a positive note even if it is only to thank the interviewers for seeing you.

QUESTIONING TECHNIQUES

How you present yourself during that all important interview is crucial. You want to convey yourself in a professional and mature manner in order for law firms to take you seriously. Remember, you've worked hard to get to this point. You don't want to mess up your interview stage because you lacked the correct technique in your interview.

REMEMBER: It's what you don't say that counts.

INTERVIEW QUESTIONS AND ANSWERS

Below I have provided sample questions that you COULD be asked during your interview. I have also created some sample responses to help clarify the type of response employers will be looking for.

Your responses to the questions are fundamental in your success, and therefore you need to spend a considerable amount of time working on your answers.

What has made you decide to apply for this position?

The interviewer wants to see a genuine enthusiasm in your answer. It is here that you would show what you can contribute and not what you can take.

> *'This job is a perfect match for my skills and hopes for my career. I know I can be successful with your firm and at the same time, my successes will be rewarded.'*

You don't have any experience in litigation, is that correct?

You were shortlisted, so this obviously isn't a problem.

> *Instead of saying, 'No, I don't,' you could say, 'I don't yet have experience in litigation, but I would love to broaden my experience in this area. Because I am a fast learner and adapt well to new situations, I think litigation would be an exciting new experience for me that I could excel in.'*

What are your strengths?

If you have done research on job position you've applied for, then you will know what exactly what the employer is looking for. Tailor your answer to fit and focus on what most interviewers seek; problem solving skills, teamwork, flexibility and motivation are all good examples to speak of.

Focus on select matters rather than list a lot of strengths. By knowing what you have to offer them, you will be able to talk about it in a way that will keep the interviewer engaged.

> *'While I do work well on my own, I do have the ability to work in a group, both as a participant and as a leader. My motivation to help people who are unable to help themselves has helped me to become better at what I do, and I know that I am very flexible.'*

What is your biggest weakness?

The interviewer is asking this question to see if you are arrogant, whether you know yourself and how you are working to overcome a weakness.

> *'My colleagues have told me that I tend to be too focused on my work and that I need to remind myself to lighten up.'*

Don't be tempted to use this question to be funny or to offer a real weakness. Besides the three reasons already listed for why this question is asked, the interviewer will ask this question because it helps them to see how you handle difficult situations.

What has been your greatest challenge, and how did you overcome it?

You should have an example ready of a situation that brought you outside of your comfort zone and how you adapted. Make sure your example is relevant to the job.

> *'While undertaking my studies we did a mock-courtroom exercise and I briefly froze up when it came time to speak in front of a crowded room. By taking a few deep breaths and thinking about my next statement, I was able to overcome the fear and continue on to win my case.'*

Where do you see yourself in 10 years' time?

This is where you show the interviewer where this job fits into your goals and aspirations. Here you would explain how the job is an opportunity for you to grow and develop as a solicitor. Never bring up goals that are truly unrealistic.

> *'In 10 years' time, I hope to see myself as an extremely successful barrister working for the QC. I believe working here, will allow me to utilize my skills and expand my knowledge to ensure that I become the best barrister I can possibly be.*

What is your time management like?

Time management is undoubtedly a skill not every possesses, but is crucial when it comes to applying for jobs. Being able to manage your time effectively is imperative to demonstrate your time management qualities and professionalism.

'I am very effective at time management. I am the type of person who is extremely organised and knows what they want to achieve during each day. I like to keep lists, which act as a reminder of what I want to achieve and in what timeframe. For example, if I have a busy schedule planned for the forthcoming week, I will always write down what I want to during that week. This allows me to plan ahead and makes sure that I have everything in place so that I can achieve each objective.'

What do you know about us?

This is another chance for you to impress the interviewer. Show them that you took the initiative to look into the company for which you are interviewing. In this case, what you know isn't as important as the fact that you know something. Referring to their annual report or how they are expanding will show the interviewer that you have researched the firm and like what you have learned.

'During my research, I found that your rate of expansion was extremely high. What this tells me is that the Chambers is successful, highly professional and withholds great reputation. This is definitely somewhere I could see myself fitting in.'

What have you been doing recently?

This type of question is not asking what you get up to in your spare time; instead it is asking what you have been doing in order to prepare for this job position.

'I have been extremely focused and motivated to improve myself in order

to make a successful career as a barrister. I have obtained lots of relevant work experience by shadowing current barristers, in order to see what their day-to-day work life entails. I have to say, I loved every minute of it, and although I didn't fully comprehend the complexity and exhausting nature of the job, I am still 100% committed to becoming a barrister, and I believe I have what it takes to excel at this role.'

Below I have provided more interview questions, which you can fill in your responses.

Why do you want to become a barrister?

Why do you want to be a member of this Chambers?

What skills do you have that you can bring to this job?

What would you do if you don't get the pupillage?

Why do you want to be a member of this Chambers?

Tell us about a recent case you have interest in.

What can you bring to the Chambers that other candidates can't?

Why should we pick you over all of the other applicants?

How did you find the BPTC?

What was the hardest thing you had to do on your mini-pupillage?

Why do you want to become a barrister as opposed to a solicitor?

What have you done so far to prepare for a life at the Bar?

ASKING QUESTIONS YOURSELF!

Generally, at the end of the interview, the employer will usually invite you to ask questions. Asking questions to find out more about the job makes you look good and is a win-win for all involved. It will show the interviewer that you are very interested and that you like to take initiative.

Below I have outlined some of the questions YOU could ask at the end of the interview:

- Could you please share with me some of the details about the Chambers?
- How would you describe the individuals who are successful in this position? What characteristics or qualities do they have?
- How will my performance be evaluated? How often? By whom will I be evaluated?
- Where will my opportunities lie over the next five years knowing my commitment to working hard and demonstrating my legal skills and abilities?
- What are the biggest challenges I would face in this position?
- What is the next step in the process?

OTHER ASSESSMENTS

The chambers will also set a legal problem or give a question for trainees to prepare and present. This includes writing a short piece of written work and argue a point as part of a final advocacy exercise. Trainees will need to use the allotted time to consider the relevant issues ahead of their discussion.

There is likely to be a discussion on the following points:

- General legal matters;
- Procedural or ethical issues;
- Cases;
- Experience of working at the Free Representation Unit (FRU);
- Mini-pupillage or mooting experience.

Some interviews will also involve:

- Role plays;
- Group tasks;
- Stand-alone written exercises.

The discussion topic part of the interview will involve half a dozen discussion topics to choose from. It will require thinking on the spot and answering questions from the interviewing panel. The interviewee will have to answer questions about the area of law that they have expressed an interest in, from their application.

It is a good idea to read some law blogs and law sections of newspapers as the interviewing panel may wish to ask about knowledge and experience of these.

KEY POINTS

- **Dress to impress.** As mentioned multiple times already, your first impression should be your best one. Unless you are informed that the interview is casual, you should be prepared to wear a suit.
- **Read your CV, Cover Letter and application the night before.** The interviewer will be asking questions regarding the content. If there have been any changes or additions since you turned these items in, bring the new information with you. Any new experience could be the difference between getting the job and leaving without it.
- **Be aware of your body language.** No matter how nervous you may be, or how stumped a question asked may have you, let them see you as a confident, clam and composed individual.
- **Greet each person you meet with a firm handshake and excellent eye contact.** While the strength of your handshake will not determine how well you could do the job, it will add to a list of things that the employer will be keeping in mind as the build their perception of you. Don't overdo it, though. Broken fingers on the hand of your interviewer will not bode well for you either.
- **From the moment you walk into the interview to the moment you leave, assume you are being tested.** This means that you should be friendly and polite to everyone you come in contact with. Always think before you speak. Interviewers want to see that you are well spoken.

- **Plan your journey.** It is important to know the route to the job interview. This will help you to get there ahead of schedule. Showing up late will not help your chances of landing a job.
- **The delivery of your answers is very important.** Excessive one word answers, as well as rambling on and on about your life will not be seen as appropriate. You want to be seen as a person who can formulate smart, concise responses. After all, you will be speaking on behalf of your clients once you land your job.
- **Know what questions you want to ask your interviewer.** It is perfectly acceptable to bring in a note of your questions. It will let the interviewer know that you have thought about the job ahead of time and that you are interested in knowing more. Make sure to listen to everything the interviewer says during the interview so that when you ask your questions you are not asking about something that has already been said.
- **Look engaged.** Sitting forward and taking control of your facial expressions and nervous gestures will be important. You don't want to be fiddling or compulsively moving your feet and hands. Steady breathing can be used to calm your nerves. Make sure you engage with all the people in the interview.
- **Smile.** Not only will smiling make you feel more relaxed, but it will help you to build a nice rapport with your interviewer.
- **Don't attempt to fill awkward silences**, especially when the interviewer is looking at your CV.
- **Make sure that you listen** to the interviewers question in its entirety before attempting to answer.

CHAPTER 12

GLOSSARY AND KEY TERMS

Within this chapter, I have provided a glossary of all of the key terms you will be expected to know as an aspiring barrister.

ADVOCACY	The act of pleading, arguing, defending a case or a position. Barristers are advocates who provide legal assistance during court cases and disputes.
ADVOCATE	A person who presents an argument on the behalf of someone else. They provide legal advice and pleads the cause of another in courts and tribunals.
ATO	Authorised Training Organisation. A recognised organisation which offers a pupillage to any suitable student upon application as a training barrister.
BAR COUNCIL	Represents barristers in England and Wales. It is also known as the General Council of the Bar, which is the Approved Regulator of Bar.
BARRISTER	A barrister is a type of lawyer involved in advocacy and litigation in courts and tribunals. They wear wigs and gowns and provide legal aid to the public.

BCAT	Bar Course Aptitude Test. An aptitude test which needs to be passed before undergoing the BPTC. The assessment is used to determine whether a person has the correct skills and qualities required to move on the Bar Professional Training Course. (See BPTC for definition).
BPTC	Bar Professional Training Course. This is the vocational stage of training barristers. It teaches law procedures, advocacy, ethics and practical skills required to become a barrister. It is the final stage of training for the Bar.
BSB	Bar Standards Board – this is the Bar's independent regulator.
CALL TO THE BAR	Like a graduation, it is a formal ceremony where the Head of an Inn of Court officially names graduates as barristers, after completing the BPTC.

CHAMBERS	The collective name for a group of self-employed barristers (sets) who share work space, staff and legal overheads.
CIVIL LAW	Law concerned with private relations between members of the public.
CLERK	A person working in court who assists the role of a judge.
COUNSEL	This is another way to refer to a barrister.
CPD	Continued Professional Development which barristers must complete every 12 months.
CPE	Common Professional Examination. This is a course that allows non-law graduates to convert their degree into a law degree.
CROWN COURT	The Crown Court deals with more serious offences.
CRIMINAL LAW	Covers every element of law misconduct. From indicatable offences to less serious crimes.

DIRECT ACCESS	Scheme which allows members of the public to contact barristers directly.
'FIRST SIX'	This refers to the first six months of a pupillage in which a person will shadow a qualified barrister and help them with their duties.
GDL	Graduate Diploma in Law. This is another name for the CPE, which allows non-law graduates to convert their degree into a law degree.
HEAD OF CHAMBERS	A senior barrister in a set of chambers who has been appointed the head.
INNS OF COURT	Four historic institutions including Lincoln's Inn, Inner Temple, Middle Temple and Gray's Inn. They are able to Call barristers to the Bar. They provide education and training for students and barristers.

JUDGE	They are impartial decision makers in courts whereby the interpret the law and assess the evidence in order to reach a conclusion.
JUNIOR	A barrister who is not part of the Queen's Counsel.
JURY	A group of people who sit in on court cases and have to come up with a verdict as to whether a person is guilty or not guilty.
LAWYER	A person who practices and studies the law. These include solicitor and barristers.
LEGAL AID	Government funding for certain cases.
LITIGATION	Is the process of taking legal action.
LLB	A type of law degree.
MARSHALLING	Work experience with judges in courts.
MINI-PUPILLAGE	Work experience for trainee barristers, usually undertaken at barristers' chambers.

MOOTING	A legal debate in which participants conduct a case in a mock style court case.
PARALEGAL	Legal work usually with a solicitors firm.
PRACTISING CERTIFICATE	Document required to practise as a judge.
PUPILLAGE	Last stage of training before qualifying as a barrister.
PUPILLAGE GATEWAY	The online application system for the Bar Council in which participants are able to find and apply for pupillages.
QUEEN'S COUNSEL (QC)	Queen's Counsel – a position of experienced and qualified barristers.
REGULATION	The requirements for qualified barristers to follow according to the BSB (see BSB for definition).
'SECOND SIX'	This refers to the last six months of a person's pupillage. You will be allowed to undertake cases on your own, still under supervision from a qualified barrister.

SET	Informal name for chambers.
SILK	Informal term for someone working for the Queen's Counsel (QC). They are known as 'silks' because of the silk gowns they wear.
SOLICITOR	Another type of lawyer. They assist the public with legal matters and represent them in lower courts of law.
SRA	Solicitors Regulation Authority.
TENANCY	An entitlement to continue to practice with a chamber as a self-employed barrister. This is usually given near the end of a pupillage.
'THIRD SIX'	If a pupil finishes their pupillage and is not invited to become a tenant, they can apply for a 'third six'. This is another 6 months practising in another set of chambers, in hope of gaining tenancy.

HELPFUL RESOURCES

USEFUL WEBSITES

- http://www.lawcareers.net/
- http://www.thelawyer.com/
- http://www.barristermagazine.com/
- https://www.prospects.ac.uk/job-profiles/barrister
- https://www.city.ac.uk/law/careers/become-a-lawyer/Becoming-a-barrister
- http://www.innertemple.org.uk/downloads/prospective-members/Inner-Temple-Prospectus.pdf
- https://www.barstandardsboard.org.uk/qualifying-as-a-barrister/
- http://www.barcouncil.org.uk/media/246249/your_career_as_a_barrister_pages.pdf

INSITUTIONS TO RUN THE BPTC

BPP Law School - London

68-70 Red Lion Street

London WC1R 4NY

Tel: 020 7430 2304

BPP website

BPP Law School - Leeds

Whitehall - 2 Whitehall Quays

Leeds. LS1 4HR

Tel: 0113 386 8250

Fax: 0113 245 5177

BPP website

BPP Law School - Manchester

St. James's Building

79 Oxford Street

Manchester. M1 6FQ

Tel: 0845 077 5566

BPP website

BPP Law School - Birmingham (New course accredited March 2015)

34-36 Colmore Circus

Birmingham

B4 6BN

Tel: 03331 228 179

BPP website

The University of Law - London

14 Store Street

London

WC1E 7DE

Tel: 0800 289997

University of Law website

The University of Law - Birmingham

133 Great Hampton Street

Birmingham

B18 6AQ

Tel: 0800 0159519

University of Law website

The University of Law - Leeds (New course accredited April 2015)

15-16 Park Row

Leeds

LS1 5HD

Tel: 0800 289997

University of Law website

The City Law School (formerly Inns of Court School of Law)

4 Gray's Inn Place

Gray's Inn

London WC1R 5DX

Tel: 020 7404 5787

City Law School website

Manchester Metropolitan University

School of Law,

All Saints West,

Lower Ormond Street,

Manchester M15 6HB

Tel: 0161 247 3053

Manchester website

Nottingham Law School

Belgrave Centre

Chaucer Street

Nottingham NG1 5LP

Tel: 0115 848 2888

Nottingham website

The University of Northumbria at Newcastle

Northumbria School of Law

City Campus East One

Newcastle upon Tyne NE1 8ST

Tel: 0191 227 3939

Northumbria website

University of the West of England at Bristol

Faculty of Law

Frenchay Campus

Coldharbour Lane

Bristol BS16 1QY

Tel: 0117 965 6261 x3769

Bristol website

Cardiff Law School

Cardiff University

Law Building

Museum Ave
Cardiff CF10 3AX
Cardiff Website

Printed in Great Britain
by Amazon

56974265R00120